# Our FREEDOM

## STORIES OF RECOVERY

Second Edition

NICOTINE ANONYMOUS WORLD SERVICES, INC.

2003

Copyright 2003, 1998   By Nicotine Anonymous®*

This material may be reproduced ONLY for use within Nicotine Anonymous, except with written permission from Nicotine Anonymous World Services

The text portion of this book is printed on recycled paper

Printed in Canada

*The term "Nicotine Anonymous" is a registered trademark of Nicotine Anonymous World Services, Inc.
6333 E. Mockingbird Ln., #147-817
Dallas, TX  75228  USA    469-737-9304

# CONTENTS

Preface ................................................... i

A New Freedom – Rodger's Story ................... ii

1. Confessions of an Ex-Smoker............................1

2. No Desire to Quit.................................. 7

3. Miracle Down Under............................14

4. Steven's Story..................................   17

5. Not One of "Those" People.....................…32

6. Dippers/Chewers Need Help, Too................... 35

7. Grateful to Be Free........................… 40

8. A Deeper Faith...............................… 45

9. Hooked on Getting Healthy............................. 51

10. She Kept Coming Back................................. 54

11. A Puff Away................................... 58

12. Doing Cancer Research................................ 64

# PREFACE

<u>Our Path to Freedom</u> is a collection of personal stories by members of Nicotine Anonymous, a fellowship of men and women helping each other to recover from nicotine addiction. The fellowship, formed in the '80s, is a diverse group made up of people of all ages, backgrounds and walks of life. However, we are all nicotine addicts whether we smoked tobacco or chewed it. In the Nicotine Anonymous program,[1] many have found freedom from the compulsion to use nicotine as well as greater serenity and happiness.

In preparing this book, we sought to represent the diversity of our membership and to retain the voice and meaning of each author's story. In 1990, the fellowship changed its name from Smokers Anonymous to Nicotine Anonymous. Some of the stories referred to Smokers Anonymous. These references were changed to read Nicotine Anonymous for consistency.

The Promises[2] of our program speak of "our path to freedom, joy and serenity." It is our hope that the reader will benefit from the sharing of our stories on his or her path to freedom.

*Nicotine Anonymous*

---

[1] The program is outlined in <u>Nicotine Anonymous: The Book</u> available from Nicotine Anonymous World Services 419 Main Street, PMB# 370; Huntington, Beach, CA 92648.

[2] "Our Promises," a pamphlet, is also available from World Services.

# A New Freedom
# Rodger's Story

*Rodger F. is one of the co-founders of Nicotine Anonymous. This is his personal story of recovery from nicotine with historical information on the start of what today is known as Nicotine Anonymous.*

I would look down and realize I had two lit cigarettes burning in the ashtray. The burning tip of a cigarette would fall into my lap as I drove a car. I would have a cold and take cough syrup just so I could calm down my throat enough to smoke a cigarette. If I knew you were a non-smoker, I would take my car instead of yours. I was addicted to nicotine.

I lived to smoke. But I would never admit that to myself or to anyone else. However, 50 to 80 times a day I went through the ritual of patting pockets for my pack, tapping out a cigarette, pulling it out, and gripping it between my lips, finding and striking a match, and, finally, blessedly, dragging on that cigarette. I would feel the raspiness in my throat, the almost immediate sense of relief, that pressure in my lungs. Often I would tilt my head back and exhale as if I were expelling a deep and satisfying breath. Then, depending on how low my nicotine level was, I'd either puff furiously to inject the nicotine into my lungs and eradicate those sensations of physical deprivation, or if I had just had one, I'd leisurely play with it or use it as security stick. I loved to smoke.

I used cigarettes to take the edge off all my emotions, including nervousness, fear, love, stress, and even happiness. Cigarettes were an integral part of my persona. They were part of my self-image. I saw myself as a movie star, talking with a cigarette hanging from the corner of my mouth. I wanted to be a film noir character, excitingly doomed; standing there with a cigarette in my hand and a swirl of smoke surrounding me like the movie poster for Chinatown. I reacted to music with my cigarette. I emphasized my words with a cigarette. I culminated sex with a cigarette. Smoking was simply what I did and who I was.

Phones rang, cars started, non-smoking lights on airplanes went out and I would light up. My friends never forgot that I was a smoker. They knew, they remembered.

How did I ever get to that point where my addiction to nicotine had so consumed my personality and me?

Probably, I was born a nicotine addict. My mother smoked through her pregnancy and I am sure I was first addicted in the womb. Of course, I have no memory of this. I do remember those long trips with my two older sisters in the back seat and myself between my mother and father in the front. No one thought of second hand smoke then, as my mother filled the car with her smoke and kept the windows rolled up to keep out the cold but clean North Dakota air. My father quit smoking in his early thirties and except for one smoking lapse during my childhood; I do not remember him as a smoker.

My mother, however, was a smoker. I remember the cigarette smell on her clothes and hair and all over our home. She was young then and no one questioned her smoking. I think I grew up thinking smoking was a natural thing to do.

When I was 15, we lived next to a family with four boys who were my friends. One named Ralph was the black sheep of the family and it was he who, over the backyard fence, introduced me to cigarettes. It was no big deal. Ralph made it seem rebelliously cool. I think at first I was a little nauseous, but that soon passed, replaced by that sensation of the drag, the long, wonderful drag on a cigarette.

In the small Oregon town where I then lived, there was a cigarette machine outside a gas station that closed at around nine every evening. After the attendants left, I would arrive with my quarter—the cost in the late 1960s—and buy my pack.

I smoked through high school. I demonstrated an addictive personality in other areas as well, using everything from alcohol, to drugs, to girls. I was and am one of those people who, when something has a pleasurable effect on me, must use it to the point of abuse and addiction. Until seven years ago, I had not drunk caffeine for 18 years. Then one morning, I arrived for a job interview. I was tired, having just returned from the East Coast. The receptionist told me it would be a few minutes, and asked if I would like a cup of coffee. It seemed like a good idea at the time, which is also one of the recurrent themes of my life. I had the cup of coffee, I did the interview very well and, even though I was nervous, I got the job. Caffeine worked for me.

A year later after a really busy day of appointments and meetings I went to my doctor around five in the afternoon. He took my blood pressure and frowned. "You've got high blood pressure. I may have to put you on medication."

I replied, "That's impossible. I've always had low blood pressure! I'm a runner! I've never had blood pressure problems."

The doctor was not impressed and told me to return in 30 days to recheck it. I went home expecting to die shortly. I returned 30 days later in the early morning anxious to hear the bad news. The nurse came in, took my blood pressure, and asked me the reason for my visit.

"High blood pressure of course!"

She looked at me curiously and said, "You've got low blood pressure."

The doctor arrived, puzzled, and began asking questions. Finally, he asked, "The previous time you were in, did you drink any caffeine that day?"

I thought, "Yes, probably about five double espressos, three cups of coffee, and maybe a coke, why?"

"And today?"

"Nothing this morning."

"I think we've found the problem."

I am an addict and I smoked addictively. I smoked through high school as much as I could. On my own while in college, I gave free rein to my smoking. I started smoking over one pack a day and then over two. It was the late 1960s and I took amphetamines, studied, and smoked. I drank and smoked. With everything I smoked. I smoked and saved the coupons that were inserted in the packs. I joked that I was going to use them to buy an iron lung. Later, I changed brands. When in Europe, I smoked European brands—at first the ones with filters and then unfiltered. Back in the United States, I found an equivalent non-filtered brand. As a non-filter smoker, I developed the yellow stains on my smoking fingers and picked tobacco out of my teeth. I remember I sniffed my finger at any time and smelled that strong tobacco odor.

In 1977, I began a spiritual journey of recovery in another 12-step program that continues to this day. Unfortunately, my smoking increased, often surpassing four packs a day. The meeting rooms were smoke-filled, and people told me not to worry about my smoking that there were more pressing problems. Thus I smoked incessantly. During a meeting I could finish a pack. If I went to lunch or dinner, I smoked up to the arrival of my salad, and then had a couple quick ones before my entree arrived. I became a life support system for a cigarette.

After I had been in that program for about a year, I was talking to a newcomer who did not smoke. I started telling him that it got better, but was stopped by a spasm of coughing. The newcomer looked at me as if I was crazy, like I was killing myself. I had a moment of clarity and realized that I was crazy; that I was killing myself, and that my recovery was far from complete.

I had had a cough since my teens. I had heard the doctor's warnings for a decade. Still I could not quit. Each year I made a New Year's resolution to quit by the end of the year. Each year I failed.

About that time, I went to marriage counseling with my first wife. At one emotionally threatening point, the counselor asked me a question. I paused, began drawing a cigarette from my pack. Then the counselor put her hand on my arm and asked, "Can you wait with your cigarette until after we've talked about this?"

I replied, "Of course." I hid the rage I was feeling. I wanted that cigarette, I wanted the time it would buy, the relief it would provide, and the nicotine-induced comfort. I responded curtly, and then excused myself to go to the restroom. There I smoked several cigarettes in resentment against the therapist who was sitting in the other room making a dollar a minute. Again, there was a moment of clarity when I realized that nicotine really did something for me emotionally.

I had always heard that smoking was a nasty little habit. With willpower anyone could quit. But if it was just a little habit, why did I seem to always be, minute by minute, obsessed with smoking? I began to realize it was not a little habit but a major addiction.

A good program friend of mine, Al B., called me at work one day. I liked Al because he smoked like me. I never had to hide the extent of my smoking from him because he was as badly addicted as I was. We talked for a while before he told me he had some material on a smoking cessation program and would I like to go to one of their sessions with him. I don't know why but I said yes, and off we went.

At the first session, facilitators described their smoking cessation program and afterwards, prompted by Al, I signed up. After six weeks of classes and a fairly earnest effort, I quit smoking. I graduated. I took up running and became obsessive about that. Then there was food. In the next months, my fiancée and I moved to a distant town in Southern California where I started a new job. We were going through many changes and one day we argued.

My reaction was to drive to a little market and buy a pack of cigarettes. I began to chain smoke. I drove into Los Angeles and met Al for lunch. He was surprised to see me smoking and told me to throw the remaining half pack away, which I did. What occurred to me was that after six months of not smoking, when a certain situation had come up, I had absolutely no defense against the first cigarette. There had been no thought about it. I drove, I bought, I smoked.

However, the next day my mind started working. What it told me is that I had smoked a few, but then had thrown away the rest of the pack and not smoked anymore since. Maybe I could control my smoking. That day I smoked a couple. Four days later, I told myself I could still go six hours without a cigarette. A month later I was smoking a couple packs a day. It was another hard lesson. With the first cigarette, I was a hooked again. It wasn't the first pack; it wasn't after the first week. It was that first cigarette that made me a smoker, when I traded non-smoking for renewed addiction to nicotine.

Years later I remember a conversation with a friend who had quit smoking and become a runner. However, he admitted to me that recently he had started having an occasional cigarette. I said, "Oh, so you've become a smoker again?" He contradicted me saying that I didn't understand that he only had a cigarette once and awhile. He wasn't a smoker. I replied that my belief was that he definitely was a smoker again. It came with the first cigarette. Several months later when he was smoking a pack a day, he agreed with me.

After my slip, I smoked heavily with a maximum amount of guilt. One friend, Dan H., asked me to help him quit smoking. I waved a cigarette at him and told him it hadn't worked. Stephanie S. told me I should start a Smokers Anonymous meeting. I replied that she must not have noticed I was smoking again. Finally, Betsy, an older woman, asked me if the smoking cessation program ever sent me their newsletter. She would like to see it. When it arrived, I took her the literature. She was so happy that she insisted that we both go to the next session. I was too much of a people pleaser and liked Betsy too much to disappoint her. We went. Betsy railroaded me into signing up again.

After six weeks, I quit again. This time it was different. The first time had been easy, a honeymoon. This time it was difficult. It was a nightmare: cravings and obsessions coupled with physical problems. I had narcolepsy, falling asleep uncontrollably, especially behind the wheel of my car. I could barely drive.

Over the years I had learned some lessons in my attempts to quit, especially in my other program. I had no defense against the first cigarette, nicotine was cunning, baffling and powerful, and, most importantly, I had to give it away if I wanted to keep it.

I tracked down Dan and Stephanie and told them they were going to quit. I served up a mixture of the smoking cessation class and a twelve-step program. We met in restaurants once a week. Sometimes we had a few people. Sometimes I was the only one who showed up. After a few months I was feeling great. I was feeling liberated from my obsession with cigarettes. I found that God could do for me what I could not do for myself,

I was running. As a smoker, I had always assumed that you ran until your breath was gone. I soon learned that I could run until my muscles said stop and still have plenty of breath. That was a tremendous point of gratitude for me, coming into contact with, and appreciating, a body that I had abused for so many years.

Significantly, I decided to commit to giving it away, to help others quit smoking. After several months, four of us were together on a Sunday afternoon on Venice Beach. Dan, Rob K, and I had quit while Stephanie was trying. We decided to start a meeting and call it Smokers Anonymous. The next week, late June 1982, we met at my apartment in Santa Monica. There were maybe a dozen people. Two weeks later Maurice Z. came and quit. He was to be one of the most important people in the early years of our fellowship. Others came to our discussion meeting where we ate popcorn and drank sparkling water. Soon it was too big for my living room and we moved to a room in Roxbury Park in Beverly Hills.

I was being of service and trusting my higher power and it worked. I have not had any nicotine since February 17, 1982.

Those first years were exhilarating. I had a high volume of phone calls every day. We made many mistakes. At first, we decided that one of the steps did not apply to smoking and we became temporarily the first 11-step program. Maurice, an author, wrote an article for *Readers Digest* that was published in May of 1985. Thousands of letters poured into the post office box I had borrowed from a friend. In fact, the volume of letters forced him to get a new box. We had no literature so we put together a letter and a meeting format, and some of our phone numbers. For weeks, the members of our Roxbury Park meeting stayed long after the meeting ended, in order to respond to all the letters. We lined up tables and created an assembly line for folding and inserting packages to potential - members.

One of the letters we received was from David M. announcing that he was a member of a Smokers Anonymous meeting in San Francisco that had started two years earlier. We also discovered that Georgie S. together with Doug H. had recently started a non-smoking meeting for Alcoholics Anonymous members in the San Fernando Valley. She had recently moved from New York where she had attended meetings there for AA members who were using the 12 steps to stop smoking. Shortly thereafter the San Fernando meeting became a Smokers Anonymous meeting.

Within a year, there were a hundred meetings.

The article in the magazine also created controversy. At least two correspondents were from people claiming we had infringed on their legal rights. One claimed that he held the national trademark to Smokers Anonymous and another group claimed to have the California registered business name of Smokers Anonymous World Services. It was David M., who in his calm and spiritual manner, talked to the Smokers Anonymous World Services people and eventually resolved the problem. The conflict with the party that had the trademark continued until the Phoenix conference in 1990.

In 1986, the Northern California members proposed a conference to be held in Bakersfield, California. Thirty-five people from Northern and Southern California came to celebrate our newly formed fellowship. We had workshops. Bill H. from San Francisco questioned whether we were truly a 12-step program; the general consensus was that we were. Through the fellowship of our program, the 12 steps, and a belief in a power greater than ourselves, we had overcome an addiction over which we had thought ourselves powerless. The next year, there was a second conference in Monterey at which Maurice Z. became our first main speaker.

In those first years, the San Francisco groups established the first intergroup and started using a small room at the Drydock, a 12-step clubhouse, managed by David M. as their base of operations. Learning from the Northern California experience, the Southern California groups also formed an intergroup with Georgie S. as the first chairperson. Some years later, Georgie moved to San Francisco where she became involved in the program there. She and David became our first Smokers Anonymous romance that led to marriage.

I had become friends with a number of the San Francisco members, especially Bill H., who founded our newsletter, *Seven Minutes.* One day he and I were attending another 12-step program meeting on Guerrero Street. When we were leaving, Bill said that he had been thinking that we should start up a World Services organization. I told Bill that starting a World Service organization sounded much too grandiose. But Bill persisted and with the Northern California Intergroup laid plans to establish a World Services organization at the next conference scheduled for San Francisco in May 1988. This was the first World Services conference. It was during those three days that we established the organization that continues to function to this day. Being elected as the first chairperson of Smokers Anonymous World Services was a tremendous honor for me. Julie W. was elected secretary and Elizabeth D., treasurer.

The next year was an extremely exciting year for all of us. We were putting together an organization that was supporting an ever-growing membership and number of meetings. There were policies and procedures, bylaws, and literature to be written. We had growing pains and arguments where people walked out of meetings in anger. We made mistakes but then tried to make immediate amends and rectify them. People dedicated hours and hours of their time in service to help our fellowship grow and reach more and more addicts.

Personally, I was burning out and had an inflated sense of my own importance. I have heard many people who were founding members of our fellowship describe the same feelings. For a number of years, I was simultaneously the chairperson of World Service and the chairman of the Los Angeles Intergroup. I felt I had to hold all these offices and do all that work because the program needed me. I was surprised when I finally opened up the intergroup chair to elections and was promptly replaced. What I found was that a power greater than all of us directs and guides our fellowship, not myself or any other person. We are all indispensable and completely dispensable at the same time. Just when I think my latest project or job will fail if I'm not there, someone comes forward and takes it to a new level.

In 1990, we held our first conference out of California, in, Arizona. For the year preceding the conference Jack C., a founding member of Smokers Anonymous in Orange County, and I had been working with a trademark attorney to try to resolve the dispute with the person who held the national trademark for Smokers Anonymous. Jack, a former World War II Marine Corps fighter pilot, wasn't about to surrender and neither was I. We came to the conference with various options on how to continue the battle and wrestle the name Smokers Anonymous from the person who held the trademark. Then both of us in the heat of the discussion in Phoenix on this issue came to a realization that we had to quit fighting everyone and everything. For legal reasons and to clearly and exactly define who we were, our group conscience came to the conclusion that we needed to change our name to Nicotine Anonymous. It was a real change in thinking that stirred a lot of emotion. People were attached to our former name. However, we were addicted to the drug nicotine, not just ex-smokers. We were nicotine addicts.

There has also been great sadness for me. My mother who smoked through my infancy, finally quit at the age of 62. I was so happy for her and hoped I had been a positive example. However, some years later the damage done during a lifetime of smoking appeared in the form of emphysema. It progressed slowly. By the time I brought my first baby boy to meet his grandmother, she was using oxygen fairly consistently and would sit by the kitchen table with her tank and mask. My youngest boy only met her once when he was six months old. In October of that year, my mother contracted pneumonia. I flew to her immediately. She lasted three days. The doctor said that with the emphysema, her condition was not very hopeful. I stayed with her almost constantly those days. We talked and I tried to comfort her with her pain. She said, "I really wanted to see your boys grow up," and "Where did all the years go!" She went into a coma. On Tuesday morning, after I slept in her room all night, the nurses told me it wouldn't be long now. I called my sisters, my father, and my mother's minister. They all arrived. We stood in a circle holding hands with each other and my mother. While we said the Lord's Prayer, she passed away. God be with her.

Her death certificate read pneumonia, but without the emphysema, she would have survived. Her mother had lived into her early nineties. I am convinced that without smoking and nicotine, my mother would have lived to see my children grow up.

My sons, Jordan and Matthew, are two of the greatest blessings of my life and they are blessed with a healthy, active and involved father. They rarely if ever are around cigarette smoke and they have never seen their father smoke, which will greatly reduce their own risk of becoming addicted to nicotine.

I love those boys. I love this program.

Over the years we have grown. Many have been disappointed that we haven't grown larger faster. It seems that only a fraction of our members keep coming back and get into service. Many, if not most, use our program to stop smoking and then disappear. It is sometimes discouraging for those of us who are of service. What I know is that, for me, stopping smoking was not the answer. I have an addictive personality. Left to my own devices I will return to my addiction. My experience with coffee tells me that. Even if I think I will never smoke again, why take the chance? I have been given so much physically, emotionally, and spiritually from this program that it only seems natural that I continue to go to meetings and be of service so that I can keep what I have found here.

Today I have respect and regard for my body and a desire to live a healthy life for as long as God allows. I have taken yet another step away from the addictive nature of my personality and toward a compassionate humanity. I have been blessed with a new freedom.

# Confessions of an Ex-Smoker

*Unable to stop, he found hope and help in one of the first groups of the fellowship. His story first appeared in Reader's Digest, May 1985, and was instrumental in bringing together two independent groups in California to form what became Nicotine Anonymous.*[3]

"My name is Maurice Z. I am an ex-smoker. I haven't had a cigarette since July 4, 1982!"

Last October, I spoke those words to thirty-two members of Nicotine Anonymous, which meets once a week in Roxbury Park, California. As the leader that evening, I called on those present to tell why they had smoked and how they had stopped. In this way we help each other through the emotional crises that ensue when the addiction to nicotine is broken.

For make no mistake about it: smoking is an addiction. We ex-smokers have discovered that smoking could not have done so much to us if it first had not done so much for us. We know about cancer and emphysema and strokes. But we also know the benefits of smoking.

Many of us are shy and nervous, and have used cigarettes as a smoke screen to protect us from intimacy. We have needed the calming effect of inhaling and exhaling cigarette fumes during tense business conferences or personal confrontations. We have discovered that when we stop smoking, powerful resentments suddenly surface and drive us up the wall. And that is mostly what we talk about at our meetings, which we modeled on the principles of Alcoholics Anonymous.

---

[3] Reprinted with permission of the author's estate from the May 1985 Reader's Digest.

## Confessions of an Ex-Smoker

After 40 years of smoking from two to three packs of cigarettes a day, after being warned by a surgeon that smoking was destroying my larynx, after being warned by other doctors that I was at risk of both lung cancer and emphysema, after suffering a mild stroke, after all this and more, I was still compelled to smoke. <u>Had</u> to smoke. And I became resigned to the fact that I'd go on puffing, coughing and spitting, despite knowing that it was killing me, until death in fact did me part.

You see, it isn't quitting that's hard. As Mark Twain once said, "It's easy to stop smoking; I've done it thousands of times." The hard part is: How do you go on living <u>after</u> you stop? And how, for heaven's sake, do you <u>stay</u> stopped?

And so, I'm here to tell you – those of you who are still killing yourselves with nicotine – that it <u>can</u> be done. It can be done as I and others are doing it right now. We don't do it with willpower. Quite the opposite. We surrendered.

We admitted that we were powerless over those dumb sticks of white paper filled with chopped-up weed. Some of us believe in God. Others rely on the strength of the group. But all of us believe it is the <u>process</u> of helping smokers still in the throes of the addiction that has been most beneficial. This is a new movement in the war against cigarettes, and it works.

Three times a month, on Monday evenings, we have a Quaker- like meeting during which each of us speaks for a few moments. We speak of the joys of tasting and smelling food, of driving a clean automobile, of how kisses taste without smoke on the breath. We speak of how our complexions have improved, of how young we feel, of the new strength we are bringing to our favorite sports. We even speak, some of us, blushing, of how our sex lives have livened up.

On the fourth Monday, one of us talks for a full 30 minutes. We tell our smoking autobiographies. This was easy for me because I remember it all so well, all the way back to my first cigarette. I was a shy stuttering kid of 16, on a double date with my best friend. Eddie already smoked. A year older than I, he was a man of the world. With his swagger and wide-brimmed fedora, he looked like a Hollywood reporter. I, too, wanted to dangle a cigarette from the corner of my lips, tilt my hat back, and hunch at the typewriter as I knocked out a story.

By smoking I could become Humphrey Bogart or Clark Gable. Yes, I was buying a dream when I bought my first pack of cigarettes for 15 cents. Smoking that first cigarette put me into overdrive. I could talk, laugh, even make passes at my date.

Smoking was also an act of rebellion against my parents, who prohibited the use of tobacco. While I lived at home, my smoking was clandestine. I concealed cigarette packs behind my books and hung out with other young "criminals" who smoked.

By the time I had finished college and begun working on newspapers, the smoking habit had worked itself into every part of my life. Without my daily ration of cigarettes, I could not write, eat, sleep, make love or even have fun with my children. Above all, I could not talk to people. I don't mean just famous people, or strangers at cocktail parties. (Oh, how that smoke screen helped overcome my embarrassment!) I also mean my family and friends. Every single activity in my life was fatally locked into the nicotine addiction. A nervous, high-strung character, I truly believed that a cigarette calmed me down, helped me get through stressful periods and also enhanced moments of pleasure.

Which is why millions of us find it so hard to stop smoking. Which is why, for most smokers, warnings on cigarette packs don't work, and doctors' warnings don't either. One of my best friends was a tough, aggressive lawyer named Joe A., an ex-marine and a top athlete. To cope with tension, Joe smoked three packs a day. Naturally his health deteriorated, so much that he had to take early retirement. Even after emphysema made it all but impossible for him to cross a room, he kept smoking. At age 61, he developed lung cancer.

## Confessions of an Ex-Smoker

During the last few weeks of his life, I visited Joe several times a week. All I could do was look into his sad blue eyes and think of how this wasted human being had been robbed of his vitality by cigarettes. I took the elevator downstairs and hit the street, and do you know the first thing I did? I took out a cigarette, lit up, inhaled deeply and went through the usual spasm of choking and coughing. After witnessing the disintegration of a man I loved, I still couldn't stop smoking. I felt doomed.

What happened on July 4, 1982, that finally made it possible for me to put away the deadly sticks?

I believe it was an almost spiritual sense of my own helplessness. For two years I had suffered from chronic bronchitis and a practically permanent cold. For months I had been conscious of a gradual draining of energy – mental and physical. I blamed it on the Los Angeles smog, on lack of exercise, on overwork. I blamed it on cigarettes.

I got into my car and started driving to a party. I could not make it. I turned around and pulled back into the subterranean garage of my apartment building. I switched off the ignition. I believed that I was soon going to die or, worse yet, go on living as a cripple. I had no willpower left. I closed my eyes and whispered, "God, if there's any purpose to be served by my living, please help me."

Almost as if I was in a trance, I went up to my apartment and put away the ashtrays. I threw out a half-finished pack of cigarettes. I went to the store and got a refund for the packs still in the carton. If I had stopped to think, I would not have gone through with this. I was sure – as I've discovered most ex-smokers are sure – that it was impossible for *me* to stop smoking. So I didn't make any resolutions. I just knew that if I smoked cigarettes I would die. And I did not want to die.

The Fourth of July went rather more easily than I had expected. I talked to friends on the phone, watched television, read. On the second day, I had a sip of coffee whenever I wanted a cigarette. I telephoned a friend who had stopped smoking and asked him to help me remain an ex-smoker. He was delighted, and gave me several suggestions.

By the fourth day, I was getting nicotine-starvation urges every thirty minutes. But I was staying clean. And, gradually, I felt calmer. The changes, as the weeks went by, were miraculous. My coughing and choking cleared, and those dreadful racking catarrhal spells that woke me up dozens of times at night disappeared. Gone were the chronic bronchitis, the laryngitis, the perennial bad cold.

The Los Angeles smog hadn't cleared up, but my lungs surely had.

Yet I was still fighting the urge to light up a cigarette. At this point, I heard about Rodger F., who had started informal meetings for people who wanted to stop smoking. I phoned Rodger, and he invited me to his home in Santa Monica. There, for the first time, I could share my own anxieties and symptoms with others who were suffering what I was suffering.

A 34-year-old salesman from North Dakota, Rodger had become a heavy smoker at age 15, and he says that living was just something he did between cigarettes. At 30, he was dying. But his efforts to stop smoking failed.

Then a friend, a fellow member of Alcoholics Anonymous, was told to stop smoking because she had a pre-emphysema condition and heart problems. Rodger went with her to a smoking cessation program. This time, he was able to stop. Realizing that he had succeeded because he was concerned for a friend, Rodger decided that the way to help others stop smoking was to do for them what alcoholics do to help other alcoholics.

A few weeks after getting involved with Rodger and my fellow ex-smokers, I flew to San Francisco to interview Lena Horne. Would I be able to talk to her without smoking? I did! Would I be able to write without smoking? I could! When I opened a window, took a deep breath and inhaled air instead of smoke, I knew that my fears were hobgoblins that had vanished.

Am I home free? I don't know. But I'm not taking any chances. I still attend meetings. They are like premiums on an insurance policy. I need to be reminded that there's no such thing as "just one puff" or "just one cigarette." We ex-smokers tend to forget all too quickly how truly gruesome our last months of smoking were.

These days, on summer evenings when a meeting is over, I go out to my car and breathe in the heavy odor of night-blooming jasmine. Yes, that is another thing that happens when you stop smoking.

You can smell the flowers!

# No Desire to Quit

*Although life with cigarettes was horrible, she had no desire to quit. Then it occurred to her that maybe her God wanted her to stop.*

I started smoking when I was fifteen years old and smoked for over seventeen years. Before I had ever started, I can remember trying to talk my boyfriend into quitting because I didn't like the smell of his cigarettes. Later he and I began what was known around my high school as "hobo smoking." He would inhale the smoke into his mouth and then blow into mine, then I would inhale it. I "smoked" this way for several months before I ever lit one of my very own. I believe I was addicted before I ever bought my first pack. I can remember getting really angry with my boyfriend when he wouldn't give me any smoke. I must have become a nuisance to him, because he finally told me I was grown up enough to buy my own. So, I did. I smoked about a pack a day for the first few years.

I used cigarettes for two main purposes: first, to hide my emotions; and secondly, to allow me some control over my compulsive overeating. Cigarettes very quickly became my best friend. I could feel better instantly just by lighting up. What seemed like a miracle to me at the time, I had finally found a way to stop my eating binges. I loved smoking. I thought it was the answer to all my problems and it was really working for me.

I smoked with a passion for the next seventeen years. In many ways smoking controlled my life. I chose my friends by how accepting they were of my addiction. If they didn't allow smoking in their home, I would not visit them. If they expressed concern, I convinced myself that if they really cared about me they would get off my case. Other smokers were my favorite people. Cigarettes dictated where I could go and what I could do. Movies were a problem. Two hours without a cigarette?? And church? Well, the shame of being seen smoking in the

## No Desire to Quit

parking lot, combined with hours without my drug, was intolerable.

I found that swimming became difficult, but running, aerobics and climbing stairs were just plain impossible. Going on long trips with people who did not smoke became shameful for me, too. Nobody goes to the bathroom that many times. They had to know I was just stopping for smoke breaks. After a while, smoking was banned in my office. I began lying there, too, hiding in the bathroom or the stairwell to smoke. My lunch breaks became back-to-back cigarettes, usually ten to twelve in that hour alone. My favorite place to be was alone in my car, where I could smoke as much as I wanted.

I went through several smoking cessation programs. However, I do not recall any desire to quit smoking. The sole purpose was to show other people I was "trying" to quit so they would get off my back. Sometimes I did quit for a few days or weeks. Once I woke up at two in the morning. It was pouring rain and cold outside. I was out of cigarettes. I became so angry at the idea of going to the corner store, which was not very safe in broad daylight, that I quit for a few months.

I'm not even sure what excuse I used to start again, probably my weight. I always managed to blame any weight gain on quitting smoking, but I rarely admitted that I did not lose weight when I started again. The last attempt I made at quitting was fueled by pride. My husband at the time said to me, "I don't think you *can* quit!" I figured I would show him. I went for just a few days short of a year that time without smoking. During the entire time, I had a pack hidden in the house on top of one of the bookshelves. I thought about smoking every single day. I really planned for the day I had let enough time go by to prove my point, just so I could smoke again.

As the years went by, I smoked more and more. By the time I quit this last time, I was smoking between three and five packs per day, determined entirely by how many hours I was awake. I have repeatedly lied about my smoking to doctors, family, friends and most of all, to myself. I hid my smoking as much as I could. I have stolen cigarettes and smoked other people's butts. I had to have them with me all the time, no less than two packs. I also had to have two packs of cough drops if I intended to speak to anyone. I was taking five different medications every day just so I could breathe. But, I had no desire to quit smoking. Life was like a death sentence.

About this time, I had become involved with a group of people who loved me enough to begin spoon feeding me some basic spiritual principles. I was so starved for what they had that I took all I could get. One thing they taught me that I managed to do consistently was to pray for God to show me what He wanted me to do with my life. So, I got up every morning and I prayed, "God, please show me, in great big billboard-sized letters what You want me to do. If You will help me, I will try my best to do it." Little did I know that prayer was the beginning of a long road toward the willingness to stop smoking.

I noticed things began to look different to me. I had always been able to ignore the complaints of my friends and family for the most part. Now every word they said about my smoking haunted me. I began to see that they weren't trying to harass me. They were genuinely concerned.

I had been throwing my butts out the window of my car for many years as part of my effort to hide my smoking. I had been driving the same car for the last three or four years and had never had them fly into the back seat, but they started to. I first noticed several burned holes in the carpet and upholstery. Then I started seeing them go back there and I would try to bat them back outside. God knows what was going on in front of me while I was flailing away at airborne cigarette butts. I kept this image in my mind of looking in my rear view mirror and seeing a wall of flames.

Then there were the billboards. In the past I had seen these tall, thin, elegant women with bright white teeth who I was sure were the image of everything I so desperately wanted to be. Now I began to see "WARNING: The

Surgeon General has determined that smoking . . ." I also realized that I didn't even look like those women. My teeth had awful brown stains that all the smoker's tooth polish in the world wouldn't erase. I was at least twenty pounds overweight. It is impossible to look elegant with a hacking cough.

Finally, after all this, one morning just after I said my prayer, the thought came to me that perhaps God wanted me to quit smoking. It scared me. I tried to talk myself out of believing it and God out of wanting it for several weeks. That didn't work. Fortunately, I didn't really believe God could help me with this, mainly because I had proved to myself that I couldn't do it. My idea of God at that time was that He was as limited and powerless as I was. So, I figured I will try this. I will let God help me with it. I will put forth my best effort and before long, God will give up. Then I can smoke again. So, with a huge amount of hope that God would give up on me, and just a tiny part of willingness to quit, I put them down.

I am truly amazed at how much work God did in me those first few months. None of my behavior was what I had grown accustomed to seeing myself do. I made a list for those around me of things they could do to support me. I put down real honest statements such as, "Do not tell me I *can't* have a cigarette because that will give me a reason to prove you wrong by smoking one," and "When I tell you I am going to die, please remind me that nobody has ever died from nicotine withdrawal." I bought a little kit at the drugstore with a tape, some vitamin pills and a lot of instructions about how to quit. For once, I actually did everything it said. I did want to die. I found myself crying on the way home from work every day. My feelings, both physical and emotional, came back to me with a vengeance.

This was an intensely stressful period in my life. I changed jobs, moved across town, got married, became a stepmother to a teenager and left the protective cocoon of the group who had given me so much love and spiritual guidance. All of this, combined with the grief I was experiencing at the loss of my drug, put me in an emotional overload.

I knew I needed more help and I began to ask God specifically to show me how to live without cigarettes. I found myself on the phone calling the crisis hot line to find a support group. They gave me a phone number. The next Wednesday night I sat in my very first Twelve Step meeting. The man who led the meeting seemed to tell my story, even down to the detail of taking nearly a bottle of ibuprofen every day just to ease some of the pain. There was a huge relief in finally being understood.

I have never been one to take orders. I have always wanted everything to go according to my plans and ideas or I would buck it every inch of the way. But God was strong for me again where I was weak. I found myself following instructions to the letter with no thought of how it should be done some other way. They said, "Keep coming back," so I came every week. They said, "Take phone numbers and call us." I did. Just in that bare beginning, I noticed hope was coming back into my life. This program was beginning to work.

Having uncovered my eating disorder, I gained between seventy and eighty pounds the first three months I was off cigarettes. I found myself weeping on the floorboard of my closet with a handful of options: suicide, pick a fight with my husband, eat all the food in the kitchen or smoke. I started small and tried to pick a fight with my husband. He would not fight back, so that didn't work. Then, the thought of one more option came and I remembered to call somebody. He suggested I try Overeaters Anonymous. God was still providing all the help I needed.

After a few weeks I got a sponsor. Again, much to my amazement, I did as directed. He went one by one through the Steps with me just as he had worked them in his own life. I worked my Steps hard. Step One seemed like a piece of cake as I came face to face with the others. At each one I realized I was incapable of what seemed to be necessary. Each time, God was there to help me again.

Sometimes I did not notice the help I was getting. Sometimes I felt completely abandoned. But then, someone from the meetings would call me, or I would notice that I had gone all day without even a thought of smoking, or some other thing would show me that I was not alone.

Today I have my life back. Nicotine does not control me any longer. The promises of this program have truly been taking place in my life. I no longer have to carry cigarettes or cough drops and I can talk a blue streak without coughing. I have been taken off all the medications I was taking. Within two months I no longer needed them. I now have the clarity to realize that I was indeed killing myself, and the gratitude that came with release from the need to continue dying at my own hands. I notice the beauty and wonder of this marvelous planet we live on again as I must have done as a child. Just today I noticed some red flowers by the side of the road, and the beauty of them gave me an enormous sense of peace. I allow myself to spend as much time examining the endless changing colors of the sky as I used to spend hiding in bathrooms smoking.

A lot of the worry and stress has simply left me. I am learning a lot about how to deal with my own fears and resentments. I no longer rage at people and I also don't need to let others walk all over me. I am also learning what it is to take care of myself. Simple things like flossing my teeth, eating a healthy diet, exercise and enough rest are becoming stable parts of my life that I enjoy.

I have allowed both God and other people to love me through this program and somehow in that process they have given me the ability to give love back. Not only that, but I find that the more I give away, the more I have. I am truly learning to love myself and to know that I am a unique and worthwhile creation of God. The gratitude I feel is impossible to express in words. God and the people in this program have given me my life just as surely as if they had pushed me from in front of a speeding car.

## No Desire to Quit

At the time of this writing I have had the gift of not using nicotine for just a little over three years. I still have many challenges in my life; it is by no means perfect. I often feel pain, fear or anger. But, I also feel joy, gratitude and peace like I have never known before. Today I can breathe and I am alive. I don't have to risk losing either of those by smoking. What a gift, what a beautiful gift.

# Miracle Down Under

*This Australian member depended on cigarettes to cope with life and avoid reality. In Nicotine Anonymous, he learned a new way to live without nicotine.*

My name is Stephan and I am a nicotine addict, powerless over my addiction; and free, for today, from any craving for nicotine or compulsion to smoke. It is a miracle.

I obsessed about smoking for fifteen years, whether I was in full blown practice or struggling against it. I hadn't ever wanted to be a smoker. I considered it to be a smelly, health-damaging, financially unrewarding bad habit. I looked with disdain at those of my family and friends who claimed that they could not stop. I felt contempt, not pity, sure that it was a matter of will, that they simply didn't want enough to stop. Then I discovered the pleasure for myself.

I had survived through to my late teens, and was living with several other young guys. We were typical of our age – pimply adolescents, emotionally inarticulate, interested in football, parties and girls. It was while watching a football match one evening with one of my mates that I became hooked. Our team was winning, and I was completely unable to find sufficient means to express my joy. I needed to share something that was deeper than I knew how to express, and in desperation, I took one of his cigarettes. The hit was instantaneous, and savage and somehow very satisfying. Every time I felt that need, a cigarette sufficed. The next day I bought my first packet. From then on cigarettes filled my need for intimacy.

As my dis-ease in life grew, so too did my dependence on cigarettes, my addiction to nicotine. They came to mean solace in times of grief, celebration in times of joy, companionship in times of loneliness. They came to mean relief from every kind of stress and avoidance of any feeling of discomfort. They were my disguise for my inability to cope.

I did not have a problem with smoking until I wanted to stop. I couldn't. I have lost count of the times when my resolve to stop smoking was as full as "just this packet of cigarettes." As the cigarettes grew fewer, my resolve diminished, collapsing completely as I smoked the last one, and despairingly bought another packet, renewing my resolution for "next time."

I stole from friends, resurrected butts from ashtrays and bins, lied about my addiction (chiefly to myself) and continued to struggle, without ever really admitting that I had a problem. Cigarettes made isolation a tolerable reality.

I came to the program in despair, truly at rock bottom. I was living in one small room with no money, no possessions, no friends; smoking compulsively and hating it. It was easy to look around a room full of people who knew how I felt, and admit powerlessness. Strangely, I smoked my last cigarette that night. No more struggle. The obsession was removed. I didn't want to smoke; I felt no compulsion. I knew it was a miracle when after a week, I remembered I had six full packets in my cupboard, and I hadn't thought of them.

Being without cigarettes meant owning the reality that I had avoided for most of my life. My withdrawal became obvious in my lack of emotional expression, my fear of intimacy and absence of skills for conducting relationships. I had to accept that I was riddled with fears and insecurities, and unable to share and be open. These were the things that smoking had denied. I had to be willing to let other people know about these things.

In the Steps and the meetings I find strength to face and accept, let go. This process didn't happen; it *is* happening! In acknowledging and exploring that power greater than myself as revealed to my understanding, my dis-ease is reprieved. I forget, it returns. I have reminders in those around me, my regular meetings, in service to other members, in conscious contact with that power. It is sometimes an uncomfortable process. The miracle is, I can go through it all without being struck by the compulsion to smoke.

    I have freedom, just for now. The wisdom of the program is the freedom of the here and now. That is my security; I crave no other.

# Steven's Story

*This story was originally presented as a speech at World Services Conference X in Denver. The speaker tells of living a life of misery and hopelessness. When he became willing to work the program, his life was transformed.*

I just want to savor this moment. Considering where I've come from, it is a miracle that I could be here speaking to you, a group of people coming from all parts of the country, who have such recovery and wisdom. Judi was being kind in her introduction by not saying what I was like when we first met. When she came into that group, she saw someone who was so isolated, shut down and unalive. When I finally started getting the program, she saw someone being born in front of her. She saw God's love being acted out in life. I am proof of God's love and power to transform a life, no matter how far it's gone down, and mine was down.

I thought about what a spiritual life is. What I seem to see with all of us is great courage and great strength and a healing of our wounds. I felt these things this morning at the marathon meeting, and I sensed our connection to one another. It's that feeling of deep connection that keeps me coming back. Most of all a spiritual life is about love: my heart becoming open, your hearts becoming open. Before this program my heart was shut down. I had ceased to live. My mind worked perfectly. I could tell you dates of any battle in any Prussian war, but my heart was gone before this program.

I want to give you some idea of my life. I lived with my mother for twelve years. I lived off my mother. I didn't have a job, and I had abandoned my art work which was God's greatest gift to me. So I didn't do art, I was emotionally dead and I nearly destroyed my health with eating. I became grotesquely overweight. I remember binging on smoking. The ash tray was just full of cigarettes, until I'd put one down and the whole thing would start smoking. Have you ever smelled the filters when they start burning? It's poisonous, it's toxic, and I didn't have the sense to get out of the room. I just sat there and smoked some more. That is how sick I was. I cringe thinking what that was like.

I broke every bond of intimacy I had ever had – to myself, to my God and to my fellows. They were all destroyed. Whole months, years, a whole decade of my life just got sucked into – I don't know where it was – just a black blur. I don't know what went on. Sometimes I'd sleep 14, 16, 18 hours a day, day after day, just watching television and sleeping. Cigarettes, always the cigarettes. Smoking was the link, the tie that kept that form of life together. It was the center of my life. The shame I felt for having lived like that, for having despoiled God's gifts to me, was just intolerable.

I remember I'd go out and look both ways down the street to make sure no one was coming before I'd go out to get the mail, so that no one would see me and I wouldn't see anyone else. I literally would not go out the door, out of the house for months at a time. I didn't know what the weather was like. I didn't feel anything. I lived like that for a couple of years with my father and mother.

Then my father developed Alzheimer's, kidney cancer and emphysema all at the same time. If you have ever been with anyone that has Alzheimer's, it's a nightmare if you are psychologically fit. If you are really there, it's a nightmare. I wasn't and it became a living hell. I became violent towards him, as he had been violent against me. He was quite brutal. He was an army officer and that's the way he lived. I returned the favor towards him. I'm sure that if Social Services had come and said, "What are you doing here?", I could have gone to jail. As far as the laws of God and man, I probably deserve to be in jail. It was heart breaking. My heart was broken. Everyone in the family's heart was broken. I was acting out of hatred. Cigarettes fueled that hatred. As I smoked I could feel that self-loathing. It was just like sucking it in.

My father would go out in the back yard and just walk twelve hours a day. He would literally walk until he wore the grass down to the dirt; just like he wore the

## Steven's Story

carpet in the front room down, practically to the floor, just walking and walking. He had a perverse ability to get under my skin. He knew exactly when to go off. Then I would go off. I got to the point when I realized there was some sense that once you cross a certain line there is no more reclamation. I sensed in my heart that I had crossed that line. I had done things for which I could not forgive myself. I couldn't forgive him for what he did to me, for what he was doing to me still. I can remember screaming, "Why don't you die, why don't you die?" right in his face and realizing that what I was saying was, "I wish to God that I could die with you." Every day was a living hell.

Finally, he died in the home and I remember the last thing I tried to do. I put him down; I tried to breathe breath into him. It is ironic that this program is about breath. As I was trying to breathe life back into a dead body, it was a metaphor of what my life had become, and it didn't work. The paramedics came and took him away to the hospital. There he was dead, emphysema had killed him, and what was I doing outside the hospital? I was smoking and it hit me, but it didn't really hit me, "He's pulling me to the grave." When I put him in the grave, it surprised me that I wept. I did not cry as a child; I did not cry as an adult. Viet Nam could not get me to cry, but seeing him in the grave did get me to cry. I was crying about my father, but I was also crying because I thought I was going to follow him. It was like I knew I was next.

The next five years were just one black depression, as if my father *was* pulling me into the grave. I can literally not remember what the difference was between 1987 and 1988. There was not one thing different between 1988 and 1989 and 1990. What happened those years, I do not know. ( I cannot remember what movies came out. The one thing I can remember of that whole time was that the shuttle blew up.) I felt a lot of guilt and devastation. The more I thought about it, I came to believe that I had killed my father. It just became overwhelming. I often wished God would take me some night, just give me a heart attack so I wouldn't have to get up the next morning and struggle on with this, because I knew I was not going to live anymore. There was no more life for me, so why did I keep hanging on?

Then, one night I was lying in bed. I was smoking. (I don't know how many of you smoked in bed. The sheet had all those little holes all over and I'd look over and there would be a little smoke. I'd just put it out, spit on it and go down and put it in the wash. I never once thought, "Maybe I'll do that sleeping some night and wake up in flames." It didn't seem to get through.) Like a vision, the horror of my life just finally came over me, and I knew in my gut that I could not stop what I was doing. There was always in the back of my mind, "Oh, if my mother dies and gives me all the money, maybe I could do this or maybe, who knows what." There was in the back of my mind that maybe somehow things could change. Something was going to come along and transform the situation. That night it hit me that nothing was going to change this situation. I was doomed. It was like having been given a death sentence and having them say, "Here is the execution down here, and you are going there tomorrow." It was like I knew it.

I think what precipitated this crisis was that in this whole life style I had finally lost my last friend. She had finally given up on me. She saw that any connection with me was putting herself through a living hell. Out of self-protection, she chose not to do it, and I understand that and totally forgive her for that. That night I lay there trying to sleep, and wave after wave of desolation and despair swept over me. Even the cigarettes couldn't get it to go away. As addicts you know how good we are with those cigarettes. We get enough cigarettes, anything will go away. Hit it with enough nicotine, super charge it, pull the filters off and I could knock anything out, but this I could not make go away. It would not stop. As I lay there, there was this voice. It was not my voice; it just rose out of me from the pit of my being, from my gut. It cried out, "God help me!" It kept repeating, "God help me. God help me."

## Steven's Story

The past four years have been the response to that request. I don't know who made that request. It wasn't me. I was committed to my self destruction, but the cry was heard. It was given to me to follow a path. For years this friend, who is here now, had tried to get me to go to Twelve Steps. Occasionally she even got me to go, which I bitterly resented, and she paid for it later. We'd get into an argument, "I'll teach you to bring me to one these things," and ". . . listening to Twelve Step people ramble on." She gave me the <u>Big Book</u>, and I read the whole thing and thought very arrogantly, "very poor writing." I was quite the literary esthete, "You know, Royko would never write like this. There can't be anything in this book; it isn't literature. Of what use can this book be to me?" I went through the whole <u>Big Book</u> and not one thing jumped out at me. But the seed had been planted. Somebody had told me about Twelve Steps. I had been to a few meetings. Some little thing stuck back there so that after that night of crying out to God for help, I realized, "I know where to go now. There is some place I can go with this. I know who to go see." I knew there was Nicotine Anonymous, because I had gone to it. I had gone there a couple of months before. Chuck was there and Pat was there. In my arrogance I couldn't hear what they had to say.

Powerless? Yeah, I'm powerless, but the unmanageability? I was convinced that my cigarettes were my manageability. It was how I managed my life, and they were asking me to give them up. Then my life would be manageable. That was just total insanity. What were these people talking about? They were idiots, yet they were not smoking, and there were people going into the group and getting off smoking. I just couldn't tolerate it. After a month or two I just got up and left. I walked out and didn't come back. I thought, "They don't know what they are talking about." What I knew about the program was I didn't have the courage to start in with Nicotine Anonymous. That would be the proof of "could God work or not."

## Steven's Story

I went to OA and got the pink cloud abstinence. I lost forty pounds in three months and this was great. I didn't do the Steps or anything, but just being around it was great. Then the day came when I thought, " If this stuff really works, I'm going to do the acid test, the one thing that I know I can not do. It is impossible for me, I have tried it, I don't know how many ways." Eight days was the longest I had ever done it in my lifetime, and I knew by the fourth day that I was going to go back unless I had something else. I didn't know what I needed then, so on the eighth day I picked up and smoked. I was scared to come to Nicotine Anonymous because if I walked in and it didn't work, then I was totally hopeless. I would slip back and I would be dead – maybe a gun to my mouth or God knows what. I'd probably burn to death. But I knew it was a death sentence if Nicotine Anonymous did not work. Finally I thought that OA seemed to work and it was the same Steps. It felt like maybe it was time to do it.

I just walked into the meeting. There was Chuck and there was Pat. That is pretty much why I continue to do this. I know that there may be someone that was in the position that I was in that needs to walk in and say, "This is rubbish. It doesn't work." Deep down inside they know that they are not ready and they need to come back in a year or two or three. What would have happened if Chuck and Pat were not there, if that meeting had folded? That was the only meeting in Denver. If there had not been Nicotine Anonymous, I could have done OA, but I would have smoked. I can't get off cigarettes in OA or SLAA or CoDA. It takes Nicotine Anonymous to get off nicotine. I knew that.

When I walked in, I heard this remarkable man speaking. I said, "Whoa! He's talking some stuff here. Whoa! It's just like that thing I learned in Viet Nam. It's like who has it is gonna live, who has the real stuff." My radar said he did, he had the most. He was Milton. He and I were talking and Chuck sauntered over and said, "You know, he is a sponsor, and you are looking for a sponsor, why don't you kinda . . ." There it was – another miracle. I needed a sponsor desperately and didn't have the sense to ask for one.

The first time Milton called me he said to go over to the seminary. I wondered what he was doing in a seminary. I walked in and there he was, a Catholic priest. I have a lot of trouble with the clergy and churches and stuff. I had heard him talk and he had never talked about the church or his view of what it is. He was totally program: "It's the Steps and this and this." I was really surprised. (I'm being led here. I am just walking through here.) I looked at him and thought, "Nice guy, but what is this guy going to do for me, what can he do? How can he help, what does he know? Maybe he's got it for himself." What he had was the Twelve Steps. I grabbed on to those little rafts like I was grabbing on for my life. I did those Twelve Steps as though my life depended on it.

I remember the Wednesday night I decided this is going to be it, just smoking one cigarette after another, knowing these were going to be the last, the last I'd ever get, so get 'em good. The next day I went over to my friend's house because she didn't smoke. There wasn't that smell in the air, and that did it. I remember that first day I was about five or six hours into it and I wanted a cigarette. I was about to go out for a pack, but I had been to a meeting. I had a meeting list and there was Pat's name. For whatever reason I didn't think of Milton, but I tried to call Pat. There was no answer, but a remarkable thing happened. When I put that phone down, the urge was gone. I thought, "This is impressive stuff; this bears looking at."

I think part of what worked for me was that my surrender was so complete. I was so desperate that I was open to the Steps. Essentially that was my life when I came out. I did Twelve Steps like that was the only life that I had. I was a professional Twelve Step person for a while. The main focus was on the cigarettes. I had seen Milton, and I had seen from his story that his life had been transformed. So I took it on faith that my life could be transformed, that I could do it.

## Steven's Story

I went through Steps Four and Five, through resentment after resentment, the wreckage I had left behind me. It was like *War and Peace* a couple of times over – pages, hundreds and hundreds of pages, especially the fears. I thought I was there for hours. When I started my fear inventory, they just kept pouring out. It was like automatic writing. My hand could not stop; it just flowed out. I just sat and watched this hand write this stuff out. I did a Sixth and Seventh and that was important. It was the first time I had formally gotten down and asked God for something. But that was how I wanted to live my life – asking God to guide me. The Ninth Step was a great transformation. It made me feel as though I couldn't go back anymore. I was some degree safe from the old life, because of what I did with the Ninth Step.

I remember driving up to Boulder to this family that I had lived with as a youth. They had been tremendously supportive of me as an artist, and that was the most important thing in the world. You know army officers don't tend to go for artistic sons. It's bad form to say the least. This family opened their family to me and said, "We respect and admire you as an artist, that you have this great gift." It was like a second home. I ended up slashing my wrists on their carpet, twice. Driving up there after thirty years of not having seen them I was terrified. What were they going to say? What could I say with my "Big Book" in hand walking up to the door? She thought I was selling Bibles. She said, " Go away, we don't want any." I said, "No, Mrs. Thompson, I'm Steve P."

When I was driving up there, I could barely hold on to the wheel. A voice came out and said, "You are doing God's work. There is nothing to be afraid of." I was still afraid, but I could keep driving. I could go up there and do that.

Later I went to a store that I had worked in, an art store. Letting a starving artist without any morals loose in an art store was not a good idea, because I robbed them blind. I stole from them every day. When I sat down with all the honesty I could manage, I could not figure out how

## Steven's Story

much I had taken. The minimum was maybe $3,000, maybe as much as $5,000 or $6,000. I talked to my sponsor about it. He said, "You know this is serious. They could press charges. You know this is grand larceny. Are you sure you want to do this?" He called his sponsor who said if I was serious I should go through with it.

So I drove up to the art store in my best suit and asked where Mr. ___ was. It was a new building so I didn't know where he was located. I looked into where he was supposed to be and there was a policeman. I thought, " Oh, what does this mean? What is this about?" I asked around because I knew some of the people from before. They said the owner would not be back for about an hour. I went down to the book store and just sat there for a while, just waiting. Every part of my body was saying, "Get out of here! Get out of here," but I knew I could not leave. I knew if I left, I would be back – I'd be back to smoking. I had to go through with it to the very bottom.

Finally the owner came and I went after him and knocked on the door. "Mr. ___, you probably don't remember me." He didn't. I said, "I used to work for you and when I worked for you, I stole from you. I stole a lot from you, and I am here to make restitution." It's like Milton said. They tell you what the amend is. You don't go in and say I'm willing to do this. I told him I was willing to do whatever he wanted. He just kind of sat there nodding, and I vaguely remembered that he used to drink, a lot, as I remember. Then it hit me by the way he was nodding, that he was probably Twelve Steps. He said, "No, just the fact that you came is enough." I said, " Whoa!" And as I walked out of there I thought that was great. Would I ever be able to take an amend and say that's ok? Someone gave me a gift and it is something that someday I will pass on.

I went out to my father's grave and I just wept; wept as I had never wept before, just crying for forgiveness, asking him to forgive me and hoping that I could forgive him. That was hard and curiously I connected with my own son whom I had essentially abandoned. I'd had an affair, a quick, cold-blooded affair. I was ashamed to look back at what I was, at my ability to use people. I used this woman just to make another woman jealous, had a child by her and just walked out like it was nothing. Eventually she got back in contact with me and said, "Tony would like to get in contact with you. He would like to send you some art work. He's an artist." I said sure. He sent them and I threw them away. I didn't want anything to do with him or her. I hated her. I wasn't going to let either of them in my heart.

I told Milton about my son and his mother. I said I couldn't call them. He said that I had to. I said that maybe she had changed her name, maybe she didn't live in San Francisco anymore. Milton said I had to call everyone I could think of. So I called – one ring, two, three – nothing. Then on the fourth one, "Hello." It was her. I told her what I was doing. She was glad. I talked to my son for an hour the next day. He said, "You've got a lot of guts calling me." I said, "Yea, I do." I told him what I was about. The year before last I flew out there and met him for the first time. I hope to get him out here.

Without this program, I would not have a son. He would just be some skeleton in my closet. I don't think we will ever be as close as the father-son relationship that I wanted. I'm a little old now to be starting a family, so he is the only family that I will ever have. I will never have him being three, four and five, but he is my son and we are still connected. The program gave him back to me. Without this program, I would still be running from the past.

About a year or so ago, I was sitting in my mother's house, and I hadn't worked for about eleven years. I thought that I had to go out on my own. What in the world was I going to do? Maybe I could work for a convenience store. Even they require applications. What exactly would I put down for previous experience . . . twelve years living with mother and dealing with depression? It just doesn't look good on a resume. I knew some people where I get letterheads, and they could say I had been doing wonderful work for them. I took this to my sponsor and said, "What do you think about this?" He gave me this look like 'you know better than that' and said, "If that's what you want to do, then go ahead and do that. You know it's your life, but what are you trying to do with it?" I was really kind of disappointed.

The next morning I was in the shower and wondering what I was going to do. The next moment this feeling came over me, the willingness. I thought, "I don't care what it is; it has to be based on the principles of this program. It has to be based on some kind of honesty. Whatever is going to come, I have been provided for so well, so fully. I'll trust it. I will trust whatever this is about." Curiously, I was in therapy and I was talking to my therapist about this. She said that when she was in medical school she had done a thing called nursing assistant. She said, "Maybe you could do this." I thought maybe I could. It was just like a flash. If you had listed a hundred occupations that I could do, that would have been the last one I would have chosen for anything. Yet it was the one she suggested and that light went on. It needed to be done. It wasn't something I wanted to do, but it needed to be done. My OA group was just full of nurses. One woman who was a dispatcher for a group that did home health care said I didn't have to have schooling. I did have to be committed to going to a training class, but I could start work immediately. So I did. Essentially my job was taking care of dying men.

I remember particularly the first person died within a few days. The next person I went to care for lived for three or four months. He was going through living hell, calling out to God, "Take me, take me. I am ready. Why are you torturing me?" His feet were gangrenous. The doctors were taking off toes, and I was not used to this. Yet I embraced him in a way like I wish I could have embraced my father, and I wish I could have embraced myself. I remember the last night he was alive. I knew he was dying and he knew that he was dying. It was two or three o'clock in the morning. It was curious, he was struggling and suddenly he said, "Need to get up." So I got him up on his bed, and it was the strangest thing. Suddenly he was my father and I was his son; I was his father and he was my son. It was a miracle. I had been provided a miracle to heal. I was healing from what I had done and what had been done to me. I didn't see him alive again, but there was this deep connection. There was no one closer to him. His family was like a million miles away, next to eternity. I could sense that bodily need to be held like a baby needs to be held. He wanted to be held before he died. I was blest to be able to do that.

As I sat there ten, twelve hours just watching him, I started drawing him. So I had started drawing again. From him I went to a young man with AIDS, and I drew him while he was dying. Then I went to a man with Parkinson, and I drew him. Right now I am working on lithography prints, fine art prints of these dying men.

I have finally started grieving and finally knowing what spirituality is about. I have cried more in the past four years than I did in my entire lifetime. I can cry now, something can touch me and I can weep. I can feel joy. Looking back to where I was is just difficult. In a curious way, living the way I am now is more difficult. In another way, I would not condemn my worst enemy to live the way I had been living. Today I don't have any enemies.

The self-acceptance is so great. I guess that's more than anything the feeling that I have. Before program I had this feeling of self-loathing that was just visceral. I could feel it, everyone could feel it. It went out toward my father. My brother used to say, "When I am in the same room with you I can smell the hatred between you." I could smell that hatred toward myself. I could smell it when I walked into a room alone. It was that weird feeling 'somebody hates somebody here.' Today when I look in a mirror, I can say, "I like that guy there." I can say, "I love him." I can say, "I love you." The amount of work I have gone through to get here is amazing. There is something in me that is me believing, "Hey this guy is on my side now. He is going to take care of me."

## Steven's Story

The thing about this program that is so great is the service. Doing the artwork for the Conference and helping Judi pick out the place for the Conference was nice and it feels great. I've sponsored people and I'm on phone service. It's that thing in the promises – no matter how far down we have gone, we can be of use to someone. My seeing where I have come from can be of use to someone. There is no one can tell me, "I am so far down, you don't know what it is like to be down like me." I am not going to accept that because I know better.

A close friend in the other program said something to me that has always stuck: "You do not refuse a Twelve Step request. If you need to sponsor someone, if you need to do the Conference, if you need to do whatever it is . . . You have been given a reprieve from death by the Steps, by this program. When it asks something back from you, don't just say, 'No, I'm too busy, I can't be doing this.'" If Pat and Chuck hadn't been here when I came, what would I have done? Where would I have gone? This is the last stop on the train after the hypnotism and all that other stuff. If you don't do it here, there is nothing after this. Like an easier, softer way – I've been looking for it ever since I've been in the program. I haven't heard anybody come in and say, "Hey, I found it." I know it doesn't exist.

I had a call a week or two ago and as soon as I heard the woman's voice, I knew where she was – where I was a few years ago. She was living in a little tiny apartment over on Colfax, which is a real run-down street. Her husband was an alcoholic who never talked to her. She was living on television and cigarettes. That was all she had. Her doctor had just given her the last stage of oxygen that she could have. She asked me, "Can I get out of this? Is it going to be ok?" What could I tell her? What I could tell her was what I could sense and know as a truth. I could tell her and be truthful, "If you come here and are willing and open to this program, this way of life, God can transform your life." She said, "What can I do, what can I do?" I answered, "Have you thought of praying?" On the other end I could hear this silence, like "what?" She said,

"No, I want to know how to quit smoking . . . pray?" She said she had to hang up. She did call back later that night, but I haven't heard from her again.

Spirituality for me is healing and part of what I am seeing in the healing is I am doing my artwork again. I am seriously doing a meditation practice. I meditate; it is not a blissed-out state. It brings up a lot of stuff. I am just starting to look at Viet Nam. I went to a Viet Nam Vet group and I thought I got it all out, but I'll go to the grave with it. The dreams will always be there. It's like with my father. It is a tattoo on my soul and I just have to learn to live with it. But the one thing I can do is I can do it without nicotine; I can live free. Walking down the street I hear that helicopter. There isn't a helicopter goes over Denver that I don't stop and look up. It stops me every time. I will always hear that helicopter; I'll always go back there. I don't have to go back there with cigarettes. I can do it without cigarettes.

My world was a black hole that I got sucked into and now the world is so vast. Three days ago I had no idea about you and now my world includes you. Love is a word we need to say a lot more. I love this program. I love the people in it. I love the God that has seen fit to give this to us as a tool. I am in love now. I came from a place of such emotional devastation. I don't think anyone ever thought that I could recover, and it is difficult sometimes. I have come to open myself to love again. It is terrifying and frightening and I am unskillful at it, but I am open to it. The other thing with love is what I felt here, what I felt up in the hospitality room this morning, that sense of family. The family that I grew up with was more like a concentration camp – Nazi fantasies. This family that I have come to nurtures me. I feel like I want to nurture them, to serve them.

Lately I've gotten caught up in life and haven't been going to the meeting that I usually go to. Now I feel rejuvenation and I want to go back there and see what's going on, put some energy into that and connect again. You are the family that I always prayed for. I want to

## Steven's Story

thank Rodger and David. It amazed me that you got the inspiration, the message. I want to thank you both. What do you say to someone who essentially gave me my life back, my soul, my spirit? All I can say is, "Thank you." I'm sure you often feel as I do. It was an act of God, and you are the willing servants, and yet to me it was a life saver. It's what transformed my life from a living hell to something that I look forward to. It's tough at times. You don't take out a fifteen-year chunk and just flush it down the toilet, and not have it be difficult. Today it is livable; it's a life I love now. I'm using my gifts.

There is a passage in <u>A Path With Heart</u> by Jack Kornfield that I dearly love. It says, "Out of love, our path can lead us to learn to use our gifts to heal and to serve and to create peace around us, to honor the sacred in life, to bless whatever we encounter, and to wish all beings well." In closing, I wish you well.

# Not One of Those People

*Twelve Step programs amused this capable woman. She was sure she didn't belong in Nicotine Anonymous until she couldn't stop and stay stopped.*

I am addicted to nicotine. In other words, I smoked – not "pot" or "hash," (although I smoked those, too) – just regular old tobacco, readily available at your corner store. And I could not stop. I didn't even know why I couldn't stop. God knows, I tried often enough. No words from family, friends or physician could make me stop. Of course I knew cigarettes were killing me! Of course I knew I was developing early emphysema! Of course I knew I annoyed others who did not smoke! Didn't I have the right to annoy whomever I chose, whenever I chose?

Had I been drinking from early morning until late at night, the courts or my family would have had me hospitalized. They would have had me rehabilitated and would have generally tried to convince me that doing away with myself through substance abuse is a "no-no" in our society. However, we've "come a long way, baby." Women now have an equal opportunity to succumb to a disease once exclusively male.

I had decided I would smoke until something fatal caught up with me. I had been through a smoking cessation program. I had been through hypnosis. Although I did not like the smell or taste of cigarettes, I must have liked something about them or I would have done the sensible thing and quit.

A friend of mine had quit smoking through a group called Nicotine Anonymous. I thought it was pretty funny. An anonymous group for smokers? What next? In fact, I thought all anonymous groups were pretty strange. Oh, I knew there were some nice people in anonymous programs. After all, wasn't my friend Bill in one? And wasn't he a fine fellow? I asked Bill to take me to a meeting. I stopped smoking the day before that first meeting. Bill picked me up, and I sat through my first Nicotine Anonymous meeting. It was a small group, not more than eight people. The meeting was ok, but I didn't feel any great urge never to smoke again, forever and ever, amen.

Several days later, Bill came to my house and we talked about the Twelve Steps. But I already knew about that stuff. Those were for alcoholics and druggies and all kinds of other people who had uncontrollable urges and lives. This had nothing to do with me. For God's sake, they even have a Sexaholics Anonymous! I thought these programs were an unending source of joke material. I was not like THEM. I didn't come from a broken home. (In fact, my Mum and Dad were quite fond of each other.) I had never been molested as a child; my parents weren't alcoholic and neither of them smoked. I didn't start smoking at nine or ten. I was married and had a child when I had my first cigarette. My life wasn't unmanageable. On the contrary, I have a host of friends who will tell you how capable I am. I thought I probably could stop smoking if I really wanted to and I really tried. I stopped once for eight years, and I could do it again. Or could I?

I continued going to the meetings, and I learned a great deal about my addiction. I did not smoke, but I really wasn't one of "those" people.

After about four months of attending meetings in San Francisco, I moved to Southern California. I checked around. There were no meetings in San Diego. I kept receiving mail from my Nicotine Anonymous friends in San Francisco urging me to start meetings in San Diego, but I hadn't smoked in five months. I had quit. I didn't need meetings. I didn't need any dumb Twelve Step program.

It wasn't long. About five weeks after the move, a golden opportunity presented itself for me to smoke again. I wasted no time in buying cigarettes. The first day I was smoking as though I had never stopped. Indeed, I was smoking as though I was trying to catch up from the five-month fast. Catch up, I did. I immediately developed an upper respiratory infection. My chest hurt. I was tired

## Not One of Those People

all the time. I gave up exercise. I gave up running. I gave up everything, in fact, but my cigarettes.

Somewhere in the back of my head I remembered that I did not smoke when I attended meetings. I began in panic searching for a meeting. I even considered that I might have to start a meeting of my own. Then came a letter from a Nicotine Anonymous friend in San Francisco. Ron sent me a list of all the meetings in the U.S. He had circled the San Diego meeting in red, drawn some red arrows and added a short note. It was a Tuesday meeting. I had my last cigarette on the Monday before that meeting.

There are now three meetings in the San Diego area, and I try to attend them all. One of the meetings is a Step study. I am trying to understand how the Steps work in one's life. I see others who have overcome addictions using the Steps of anonymous programs. I have taken the first step towards the First Step. Today, I looked up the word "addict" in the dictionary. It said, "To devote or surrender (oneself) to something habitually or obsessively." That certainly describes me and my compulsive smoking. That means only one thing. I am one of "them."

Does this mean I must cope with a lifetime addiction to nicotine? I don't know. I am not at all certain right now the full scope of just what that means. But I do know that I will continue to attend meetings, continue to study the Steps, try to stop thinking about myself and work toward starting more meetings so that other "social smokers" can become informed about their addiction and have an opportunity to take advantage of the healing nature of Nicotine Anonymous.

# Dippers/Chewers Need Help, Too

*Chewing tobacco had become the center of his life. Even when he no longer enjoyed it, he could not stop until he came to Nicotine Anonymous.*

The first time I put a tiny wad of snuff in my mouth, I thought I had arrived. I loved how it made me dizzy and high. Ten minutes later I was throwing up, swearing I would never try that again. Through diligent practice, I learned to spit the chew out right before I got nauseous to the point of throwing up. Now I could chew as much as anyone.

After I had been chewing tobacco for about two months, I decided that it was absolutely no good for me and I needed to quit. I made this decision early one morning with chew in mouth, nauseous, head spinning and throat dry; sporting a nicotine hangover headache from the previous night's consumption of chew. I spit out my chew, swearing it was my last. An hour later, I was chewing again.

I chewed everywhere I went and did everything a human being can do while chewing. I chewed in theaters, in stores, at work, at play, while running, playing sports, driving the car, in the shower, riding the bike, kissing, having sex, talking on the phone, writing and reading. I chewed in all my college classes. I chewed at job interviews. I chewed at weddings, funerals and even while visiting dying relatives in the hospital. I would keep a chew in my mouth until I was going to throw up, spit it out, wait until I was not nauseous and then put in another chew. I lived this way for nine years.

If I were outdoors, I would spit my chew saliva on the ground, taking no care about the people around me who had to watch. For indoor chewing, I had spit cups. It did not matter much to me that my roommates were constantly on me about leaving full spit cups around the house. I just thought they were overly picky. One roommate in college moved out because the sound of my spitting disturbed his study concentration. It was his problem, not mine. If he can't handle a little spit sound and a few full cups of spit juice here and there, to hell with him – even though he was my best friend.

Chewing tobacco was the most important thing in my life. I placed it as a priority above friends, family, lovers. There were many times I would leave intimate situations with loved ones to go be by myself and chew. In fact, I would rather be alone chewing than anywhere else. I also placed myself in extremely risky situations walking through dangerous streets late at night looking for an open store selling my brand of snuff.

Once, while overseas, I could not find chewing tobacco anywhere. A friend from home was sending me a case of chew, but how was I to live until it came? I bought cigarettes and chewed them, paper and all. I tried smoking for a couple of weeks but gave it up because it was too gross for me.

Sores would appear on my gums, tongue and the inside of my mouth. I would be certain I had cancer. This didn't stop me from chewing. If the sore was on the left side of my mouth, I'd just chew on the right side until the sore went away.

After a while, my heart started hurting. I would notice knife-stabbing pains in my chest after putting in a fresh chew. My hands and feet were always cold. At one point, I had to have painful gum surgery because tobacco eroded my gums. I was chewing again before the stitches were out, before I could eat. I really believed that because I wasn't smoking, I wasn't hurting my body.

When I started chewing, a can of chew would last about a week. After several years, I was lucky if a can lasted a day. At the very end, I was getting three chews out of a can. The inside of my mouth was like leather, and pockets had formed inside my cheeks where I put the chew. The three fingers I used to insert chew were stained black because tobacco was permanently embedded under the nails.

Chewing gave me my personality, my sense of who I was. It made me feel manly and tough. I enjoyed the fact that it grossed people out. It made me feel special. Yet something in me knew it wasn't good.

I tried every means of quitting. I would buy a can of chew, put in a big wad and throw the can away, swearing it was my last. A little later I would have to go to the store and buy another can. I did this hundreds of times. I finally learned that I did not have to go buy a new can. I could just retrieve the old can from the garbage! To stop myself from doing this, I opened the can and poured the tobacco itself into and among the kitchen garbage. This didn't work either, because I'd go back with my fingers through the garbage, lumping together enough snuff to have a decent chew.

Many times, I bet a friend I could quit. If I chewed I would owe him twenty dollars. An hour or two later, I'd be chewing and twenty dollars in the hole. I'd make the bet the next day, chew and owe another twenty dollars. So I tried making the twenty-dollar bet with two friends. If I chewed, I would owe each friend twenty dollars. After several forty-dollar chews, I gave up the betting idea.

One day I was at work, and a coworker stopped by. She had just returned from a long stay in the hospital. She had cancer and was packing up her things to go on disability leave. She saw me chewing and asked me what I was doing. I told her I was chewing tobacco. A look came upon her face, a look I'll never forget and she just said one word: "Why?" I told her I was addicted. She didn't say anything and walked away. I thought about this many times. The truth was, I didn't know why I chewed any more than I knew why that woman had cancer. It really bothered me. I didn't even like chewing anymore. And I could not stop.

A friend of mine quit smoking. I asked how she did it. She told me she had been going to Nicotine Anonymous meetings. After a few weeks of talking about it, I agreed to meet her at a meeting. Immediately after my first meeting, I went home and chewed. A few days later I went to my second meeting. There was a man there who had quit smoking. I asked him to be my sponsor. He said yes. Two days later I took my last chew and I have not chewed since.

I did everything I was told to do in this program. I went to meetings. I listened. I shared. I got a service commitment right away. (My sponsor once said, "This program – it's about making coffee!") I made a program call every day. Instead of chewing, I would talk to people, go for walks, drink water, read program literature, exercise, get to a meeting. My sponsor walked me through the Steps. I started telling the truth for the first time in my life. I found hope. I learned about prayer. In my Fourth and Fifth Step work, I found out what a selfish child I had been, and instead of dwelling in self pity about it, I changed and started to think about others. I got involved with volunteer work in the community. I began to make amends to my family members and my friends. I worked with newcomers and showed them what I had been shown.

Everything in my life got better. All the physical symptoms of the nicotine damage went away. I realized I was making friends in the program – dear friends who really loved me. And I loved them. New people would come into the program and we'd all stick together and help each other.

I never became perfect, nor did all my problems disappear. Life goes this way and that. The difference now is that I don't fight life as much as I used to. Every once in a while, I just let go and go with it. That is when I enjoy life the most. When I get off track there are people around to remind me of what's important. Usually what helps me more than anything is helping someone else. I am no saint, that's for sure, but I do find it impossible to feel bad after I have been of useful service to someone worse off than me.

Along with many other things, I am learning about faith. To me, faith means all the things within myself that I know to be true. I try to act on this faith as much as I can. Faith is what I know, and when my actions are aligned with this self knowledge I become free to be the person I am, the person I was afraid to be when I used nicotine. Every time I act on my faith, I have to trust God and let go of what happens. I've had many adventures. My life is filled with people I love. I do things I enjoy and have stopped doing things that have no meaning to me. I have fun. I believe that the purpose of life is to enjoy it, moment by moment.

Today I have a sponsee in the hospital due to a lung transplant. He destroyed both his lungs because he couldn't stop smoking. He has tubes going in and out of every part of his body. A breathing machine pumps oxygen into his donated lung. Since he cannot talk because of the tube down his throat, I talk to him. We pray and meditate. I tell him stories. I share with him like we are at a meeting. Then I leave, walking out into the open fresh air, taking in the sky, the noises, the people. He stays in the hospital bed. Why him and not me? I don't know. For some reason that I can't understand, I have been given a gift. I don't have to use nicotine. I get to be me.

# Grateful to be Free

*Her inability to stop smoking filled her with shame. She thought she would die a smoker. Freed from the compulsion, she has her self-esteem back.*

I really don't remember my first cigarette. All I remember is being a smoker by the time I was seventeen. At some point, someone must have indicated that they felt that I was addicted, because I remember deliberately not smoking for a day and smugly feeling that it wasn't really addiction, rather it was something I chose to do. I left for college and never gave it another thought.

A few years later, I had a throat infection and couldn't smoke for a week. My boyfriend at the time promised me a big reward if I could make it without smoking for a month. I couldn't make it and realized that I was dealing with something that wasn't going to go away because I "said so," and I may *not* be able to just stop anytime I wanted.

There were repeated attempts to stop throughout the sixteen years of my smoking, and I would only get a couple of days or a few weeks together and not be able to go on. It became so much work to stop that often – planning, promising, counting, fighting with my conscience and negotiating with my addiction. I was never able to stay stopped and always felt ashamed and embarrassed with my friends and family, but worst of all I always felt like a failure to myself.

Nicotine certainly is the progressive disease they say it is, because the pattern is always the same. First it would just be a puff or two. Then when that wouldn't do, I'd "grub" a cigarette or two off my friends, or strangers if need be. Feeling guilty for taking someone else's smokes, I'd buy my own pack, have a few and throw out the rest, or have someone else hold them for me. That might suffice for a week, so I'd leave the pack in my car, running out to have a cigarette and assuring myself that this was the way I wouldn't exceed my designated allotment. I always

## Grateful to be Free

managed to rationalize my feelings enough to be back to smoking two packs a day in a very short time, conveniently forgetting all the shame I had endured.

I've heard people share horror stories as their motivation to stop smoking. I thank God that my life has never been touched by any cancer, emphysema or smoking-related illness; but because of this, I was "immortal."

I loved to smoke. I could sit and relax for hours with my cigarettes, a pot of coffee and the Sunday *Times*. Smoking was a "time-out" for me. No matter what was happening to me, I could find the time to stop the world for a few minutes and smoke. I could handle anything with a cigarette in my hand.

Oh, but how my addiction grabbed hold of me! I can't believe the excuses I came up with to continue smoking: The reason I was out of breath and had no endurance? I didn't exercise. My breath, clothes and the rest of my environment smelled bad? Well, smoking is not such a bad vice; I could be gambling, lying, cheating or stealing. Die from smoking? I could be hit by a bus just as easily. At least I'm not altering my consciousness. That two week cough? It's from congestion. If the house smells bad, we'll air it out. If I burned it, I'll fix it or replace it. If you won't have me with my cigarettes, you won't have me without.

I continued smoking through my life, always feeling shameful and different. Everyone else could stop smoking, but I guessed I would be one of those people who would die a smoker. So many people nagged me, it seemed that everyone was stopping. How come I could be so successful in many ways, but I had no power over a little thing like cigarettes?

Then one day it happened. I felt the courage to pick a new date. I had done this so many times before. Could I make this one stick? I had failed every other time but I had to try one more time. On the night before my quit date, I had a "This is my Last Cigarette" ceremony. Just before I went to sleep, I had a number of cigarettes in a row. And then I had my last one. I went to the sink, soaked the remainder of the pack and went to sleep.

My withdrawal? It was typical, but awful. The first three days I felt like a ghost. I couldn't focus my mind and had no control over my body. I craved a cigarette so badly, I ached and I cried. I was irritable and emotional. It seemed that every cell of my body hurt. For weeks, I was ready to burst into tears at the drop of a hat. My friends at work wanted to tie me down and force me to smoke. I was fighting incessantly with my very supportive boyfriend. I don't think I had a good night's sleep for two months. I tossed and turned throughout the night, getting up every two or three hours, unable to sleep. During this dreaded time of transition, it took all my energy to beat down the demon within me. I felt like my soul was ripped apart and was in shreds before me. I could do nothing but dedicate every waking moment to not taking that first drag. Even during sleep, I'd be fighting dreams where I'd have smoked an entire pack.

My addiction took on a persona and had become the enemy. It tried every trick in the book to make me take that first puff. I would dream that I had a cigarette and when that wouldn't work, I would dream I smoked the *whole* pack. My eyes would find the only smoker in a crowd and would find the cigarette that landed untouched on the ground from someone else's pack. It seems that I never knew how many smokers there were in the world until I was trying not to be one! I held on for dear life, and prayed for strength. Two weeks later, I found Nicotine Anonymous, and never felt more at home as I did when I walked in the room. I found the only people in the world who understood what I was feeling, as well as strength and hope to carry on fighting the demons within me.

How do I stay "smober"? Without my Nicotine Anonymous meetings, I couldn't do it. I need the support of my group, a Higher Power and the program to remind me what I'm grateful for. I tried all the tools we learned about including deep breathing, drinking water, taking walks, making phone calls. There are times, when all else

## Grateful to be Free

fails, that I need to visualize Gail's, Rob's or Jim's face or hear their voices to keep me honest. It's amazing how I would do for someone else what I wouldn't do for myself!

I must struggle to never lose sight of the fact that I'm merely one cigarette away from having it all back. As I've been constantly reminded, "One is too many, and a thousand is not enough."

But what is so easy to be thankful for? My freedom.

The easiest things to celebrate freedom from are the most tangible. I notice the absence of a stale odor wherever cigarette smoke touched: my breath, hair, clothes, car and home. I am no longer held captive by my addiction telling me where I will sit, when I will go and with whom I'll be friends. My dentist is thrilled by the absence of stains on my teeth and the health of my gums. There are no more burns on my upholstery, bedding, clothes or fingers. There is no shortness of breath or pounding in my chest when running for a train or playing a game of racquetball. The windows of my car and home do not have a yellow film on them. My office is no longer under a cloud of smoke. My skin no longer has that gray pallor that only toxic poisons could cause. No longer am I exhausted after a normal day's work. It is hard to forget about these things, as most smokers can't hide these telltale signs, as much as they think they can.

What I must keep fresh and not lose sight of are the "non-tangibles." I don't have the humiliation of watching a mouth being rinsed out after a special kiss or the debilitating feeling of being a failure every time I lit a cigarette. I must not forget the resentment I carried when I had to be inconvenienced and banished to smoke outdoors when in a non-smoking home. I'm no longer posing a health hazard to my possible future children having to be born addicted, with poisons in their systems. No longer do I have to sabotage all my other attempts at good health and longevity, expecting that a good diet and vitamins will offset the effects of smoking. I have gained my sense of choice back. I do not have to make decisions trying to accommodate the craving for nicotine.

But the greatest gift I received is the return of my self-esteem. After lying to myself and to God every night, I finally feel unburdened, like I'm not hiding anything shameful. I have been able to restore enough sanity to my life to be able to look at "putting down" my cigarettes as embarking on a journey. It has been a rough trip, painful at times, because I chose to look at <u>why</u> I was craving each cigarette – taking a long look at the triggering emotions. I've learned so much! It's been a long road but I can even say that I've learned to like myself and I like who I've allowed myself to become. I've even let someone wonderful in my life to love me, which never could have happened if I had continued smoking. I do believe my Higher Power has rewarded me for accepting my addiction, and growing through it. Life does look great on this side of the fence!

# A Deeper Faith

*She was religious by vocation, but she developed a more personal spirituality in her recovery from nicotine addiction.*

I started smoking in high school to be cool. My mother smoked but I hid my cigarettes from her, cleverly stashing them away in my underwear drawer. Who would have ever thought of looking in such a clever hiding place? One hot summer day just after I'd turned sixteen, about one week after I'd started smoking, Mom happened to mention that she'd seen something in my underwear drawer while putting away the laundry. I was doing the family ironing and, believe me, my dad's shirt got quite a scorch that day! Nonetheless all she said was, "Perhaps you'd rather try my brand. Oh, and I suggest you not smoke in front of your father."

Dad was a rabid anti-smoker. One of the biggest fights of my adolescence was with him over my smoking. He objected not on a health basis, but because he didn't want me to be a conformist! Dad believed I was smoking to be like other kids, and he was partly right. But I also smoked to show my aloofness and disdain for my peers, an attitude that thinly disguised my fear/certainty that they wouldn't like or accept me anyway. My small circle of friends and I did our adolescent rebellion by wearing black, going to foreign films and coffee houses and, of course, smoking. We were too cool to be true. I loved smoking so much: that slow inhale, the hit of nicotine and the nonchalant exhale – out of my nostrils a la Bette Davis; out of one side of my mouth, in imitation of my mother, letting the smoke slowly float out of my slightly-opened mouth. So much cool, so many "sophisticated" mannerisms.

Once in college, smoking was a diversion during boring classes, a stimulant during last-minute cram sessions, a distraction from worry about money, grades, my family, my future and my present. Still uncomfortable around people, I could always light a cigarette and pretend I didn't care. When my father committed suicide my first year of graduate school, my mother and I consumed packs of cigarettes over stilted conversations about Dad. A few years later, during my mother's slow death from internal bleeding due to alcoholism, I was always able to step outside to have a cigarette when the feelings got too big.

I quit several times during my late twenties. I had gotten fed up with the smell and the drag on my energy. Yet I always started again, usually saying to myself the addict's favorite lie, "I'll just have this one." In my thirties, having been very active in my church for some time, I decided to study for ordination. While involved in seminary studies I visited a local convent for a retreat and subsequently decided to test my vocation in the religious order while continuing to study for ordination. My novice guardian in the order was a closet smoker, so even though I had given up my apartment, my car and much of my wardrobe, as well as my sex life, I never gave up smoking during the entire time I was a sister. My boss at the nearby hospital where I worked as a chaplain also was a smoker, so between my boss and my novice guardian I was kept well supplied. Some of my happiest memories of that time are of huddling with Sister ____ on the back steps of the convent, sharing a smoke and swapping gossip while giggling like schoolgirls.

The fact that my nun's habit reeked of smoke bothered me, so ultimately I gave up the habit but not the cigarettes! I took that cigarette habit right along with me, even increasing the amount of my smoking because I had more free time in which to puff away. I developed new rituals of my own. I never smoked before conducting a service. (I had been ordained before I left the convent.) I always chewed gum before making a pastoral call on a patient, and washed my clerical collars frequently to remove the haze they acquired from the smoke. I lit up a cigarette every time my mind started to drift to how patients with lung cancer and emphysema died.

When I came out as a lesbian and became involved in a long term relationship, my lover was also a smoker. Of course we shared a cigarette after making love. We smoked together over long, deep conversations. We smoked separately after a fight. Early in our relationship we decided to quit together. Having a partner to quit with helped a great deal. Neither of us wanted to confess to the other we'd started again.

Then came the eve of my fortieth birthday. We were sitting cozily on the living room sofa and I came up with the bright idea that I'd love to run down to the corner tobacco store, buy some "really good" European cigarettes and enjoy them "just for the occasion." That's all it took. Within a week both of us were back to our standard consumption, my lover to her three packs a day (she could smoke on the job), me to my one pack a day. We quit again a few years later – cold turkey, just like the first time.

That lasted me for five years. The first thing I did when we split up was to buy a pack of cigarettes. It was like being a teenager all over again. Liberation! I barely felt the pain of breaking up from an eight-year relationship. In my free time I hunkered down into my favorite easy chair in my new apartment, a stack of lesbian novels on one side of me, the phone, cigarettes and my favorite ashtray on the other. My favorite ways to relax were to smoke while reading, while talking on the phone to friends, before and after a good meal. Of course I often stayed up late to have "just one more" before bedtime and be overly-tired the next day at work.

By then I was doing clinical supervision with pastoral care students at a local teaching hospital. I regularly stepped out onto the cafeteria balcony (regardless of the weather) to smoke before and after a supervisory session. If a student was also a smoker, we sat together in the fog (or the blazing sun) out on the balcony just so we could smoke during the session. Never once did I question how the "smokescreen" distanced us from one another, how the rituals of smoking could (and did) distract us from addressing issues that made us uncomfortable.

## A Deeper Faith

The day came, however, when my denial about the use and effects of smoking caught up with me. I had been using smoking to jack up my energy while also blaming my smoking for my lack of energy. I had been working with the dying for thirteen years and training others to care for the dying for five years. I was exhausted, depressed and smoking more than ever. The doctors tentatively diagnosed me with chronic fatigue syndrome. I suspected otherwise. I decided I had to do whatever was necessary to regain my health, my energy. I was determined to quit smoking.

Having been a member of Al-Anon on and off for several years, I knew the power of the Twelve Step approach to recovery and I knew there were Nicotine Anonymous meetings in my area. I promised myself I would quit after my return from a one month overseas training trip. I smoked like the proverbial fiend during this trip. When I returned I took a big gulp of air, plopped down on my living room sofa and said to myself, "This is it."

Despite my addiction – and on some level, even while I was denying it, I knew I was an addict – I had maintained some level of spiritual practice up to this point. I certainly was fairly sophisticated theologically. But this was a real "crunch" moment. I knew from my own history that I could no longer do my own quitting. I felt up against a wall this time. I could see it and feel it. It was a big, tall, brick wall unscalable by my current abilities. I said, in a small voice to something that felt very big and very far off, "I cannot do this alone. I don't even know that I can do it at all. I can't bear to see myself fail at quitting again. This is way bigger than I am. Whoever and whatever you are, I need your help. I cannot do this without you. And if I do this at all it will be because you are doing it with me." That turned out to be one of the most clear and most powerful prayers I have ever uttered. Frequently thereafter I said an even simpler prayer – "Help!" – accompanied by a deep breath.

# A Deeper Faith

I went to my first Nicotine Anonymous meeting the next evening. I didn't like anyone there; I knew more than everyone there. I was deeply irritated to note some commonalities between my story and the stories I heard that evening. I was scared about saying my name, relieved to say I was an addict and then felt terribly exposed and worried about what everyone thought of me. Nonetheless, I picked up the literature and was grateful when a veteran member offered me words of encouragement after the meeting.

The piece of literature I turned to most often was "The Serenity Prayer for Smokers." This gem of a pamphlet introduced me to an approach that was utterly novel to me but that will not be new to anyone familiar with addiction recovery via the Steps. The motto is "Accept the craving." What a concept. The pamphlet and people in my meetings also assured me that the craving would pass whether I smoked or not.

Within a few days I found a meeting where I felt really at home. In fact, some of the people from this meeting are among my closest friends. This particular meeting was filled with the most outrageous humor and huge emotions. Anything was acceptable to share there. I came to count on this meeting, on the humor, the shared laughter, rage, and sorrow, as a center point in my recovery.

It was in this meeting that I first began to address my career burnout, my theological shifts, the loneliness and lostness I had tried to bury beneath the clerical role. I began dating again. Without the "cool" of cigarettes, I presented a human self that had long been hidden by both the smoke and the clerical collar. I had a place to talk where I didn't have to be wise and informed. I could fumble and bumble, cry and make wisecracks. I got a sponsor. I worked the Steps. I read the literature. I talked in meetings. I called people a lot. I changed much of my life.

The recovery process enabled me to fall apart and to come together again as a much more fluid, connected and interconnected self. It has supported a shift in my theology to something that feels truly mine and has deepened my faith. It has given me a process for ongoing recovery and shown me how essential it is to live life in community and one step at a time. Do I miss smoking? Sure, in a vague way, once in a while. Would I trade in my smobriety for a smoke? Not on your or my life; HP willing, one day at a time.

# Hooked on Getting Healthy

*Involved in another recovery program, she found that her addiction to nicotine stood in the way of more growth. In Nicotine Anonymous meetings, she found the "magic" that helped her stop using and live life on life's terms.*

I never thought I'd seriously consider quitting cigarettes, let alone actually *do* it. It was so scary, I'd put the thought out of my mind as soon as it came. But there I was, age 37, twenty plus years of smoking under my belt, actually thinking it was time to quit.

I had worked a recovery program for codependency for nearly four years. I'd grown in some really positive ways, but I could see that cigarettes were inhibiting more growth. I wasn't yet ready to admit to being an addict, but I'd learned that smoking was numbing my emotions. That, plus the fact that forty was right around the corner, made me take a good, hard look. I didn't want to go into middle age still smoking, and I didn't want to stay stuck in my recovery. I was hooked on getting healthy – spiritually, emotionally and physically!

Of course, deciding and doing are two different things! It took eight more months of pain and struggle before I could actually put down the cigarettes. I see now that every minute of that struggle, every success and every failure, were so important in getting me where I needed to be to quit and to *stay* quit.

My first move, of course, was to try to find an easier, softer way. I headed straight for the doctor for a nicotine gum prescription. He obliged, warning me that I'd still have to put the cigarettes down and now the gum, too! I figured I'd cross that bridge when it came.

My first "quit morning" arrived and I popped the gum instead of a cigarette. Not bad. I did this for seven days, gum instead of a smoke. (Pretty nonstop chewing, I might add!) Then on the seventh day I got upset about something, reached into my boyfriend's pack and smoked a cigarette. My whole week's effort down the drain! And yet I could not stop myself. Though racked with remorse

51

and guilt, I didn't give up. I did realize that quitting was not going to be easy.

Next, I contacted Nicotine Anonymous and began attending meetings. I knew, from other Twelve Step experience, it was my best bet for quitting.

I kept up the gum for about thirty days, but also smoked intermittently through that time. I knew the gum was a waste of money and hope, so I didn't get any more when it ran out. Besides, by then I'd been to enough Nicotine Anonymous meetings to know that program was the only way to go anyway.

All I could do for a long time was go and listen at meetings. I went to hear the truth about cigarettes and about smoking. I went to find the magic that would help me quit. I went to see the smiles and hear the joy from people with actual freedom from the drug. I needed to know that existed. I needed to see I could feel okay again someday.

For eight months I went with little or no success. I'd not smoke for a day, then smoke again for two. I'd not smoke for half a day, then buy a pack by afternoon. On and on it went, back and forth, up and down, as I wrestled with the demon nicotine. I'd steal them from my boyfriend rather than buy a whole pack. I'd steal one from people at work, too; or my mother, or bum one from a stranger. I still thought somehow just one more would help, would make the withdrawal easier. I finally learned that only God could make it easier. No cigarette ever could.

I also saw that I most surely was an addict, for no sane person would steal like that to hide their shame of having to use. Only an addict behaves like that. Only an addict has to use, and that addict was me.

It was a humbling eight months. Many meetings all I could do was cry. I thought the miracle would never come; I was too weak, too undeserving. But no one in the meetings ever said that. In fact, all I heard was, "Keep coming back." That much I could do. Then I started hearing about praying for the willingness to go through the pain. I could do that, too. So I did. I also agreed to show up early to make coffee for the meetings. I joined a home group. And I prayed some more.

Then on April 20, 1992, I woke up and had no cigarette. I went all day without one. And then the next, and the next.

It is still that way. I show up each day with just me and my Higher Power. No nicotine. No smokes. A miracle? Oh, yes. It is at least that. Was it easy? Hardly! Especially not at first, but the difficulty has passed. One day at a time, it's gotten easier and easier. Having the support of my meetings helped tremendously. Knowing that what I was going through was normal and typical of drug withdrawal helped too. Working the Steps helped. Prayer most definitely helped.

Living life on life's terms instead of drug-mediated has been a challenge to be sure, but so worth it. Better than I'd imagined.

I am an addict, this I've come to know. I am one cigarette away from insanity. But I also know that I don't have to have that one cigarette. There are many things I can do instead. My program shows me that I needn't even get near that insane wanting if I keep clear on God's will for me daily. That knowledge is there for the asking. Thank you, God.

# She Kept Coming Back

*Cigarettes had become her higher power. Although it took awhile to grasp the program, she kept coming back week after week and found another higher power, one that freed her from nicotine and gave her back her life.*

I smoked what I hope was my last cigarette on July 18, 1993, at 7:00 a.m. I remember it clearly – standing on the porch, tapping ashes into a soda bottle. I didn't try to make it last or savor it. I just had to smoke it and then let it go.

Twenty years earlier I had smoked my first cigarette with a friend in the woods behind her house. We stole it from her parents' stash and later lied about it. I don't remember much about how it tasted. I don't think I actually inhaled. My real smoking career began at age sixteen when I asked my mom for a cigarette so I could smoke with the adults. At first she refused, then gave in. I liked it from the start. I thought, "This is what I have been waiting for all my life."

I loved the nicotine high and smoked off and on for a couple of years until I was a senior and was definitely hooked. I began to suffer physically when I went without for several hours at school. I fell asleep in class every afternoon. Previously a topnotch student, I lost interest in school. (I could've smoked at school if I had parental permission. I grew up in North Carolina, and the schools had smoking areas for those over fourteen. I was too embarrassed to smoke at school. Only the low life types did that.)

I continued to smoke through college and then married right after graduation. The depression I had suffered for years deepened drastically. I was ill-prepared for coping with life and a rocky relationship and turned to cigarettes more and more. It seems I spent most of my days sitting at the kitchen table smoking. I also had a drinking problem. After coming close to suicide, I got into therapy and AA. I got sober, but I was still miserable. I thought constantly about stopping smoking, but felt completely hopeless. I tried the nicotine gum and stayed off cigarettes for about two months until I got stressed out. Years passed and I smoked and smoked and smoked. I was certain that if I wasn't such a bad person, I would quit.

That my life was unmanageable due to nicotine became clearer. My doctor prescribed inhalers for smoking-induced asthma and warned me of the emphysema that lay ahead if I didn't stop. I smoked in the face of two cancer deaths in my family. My grandfather died of lung cancer and my father died of mouth cancer from pipe smoking. (My family is full of nicotine addicts. My grandmother did snuff. Fortunately, most members are abstinent now.) I spent money on cigarettes that I needed for other things. I smoked in my cats' airspace. Worst of all, I suffered a miscarriage after developing a condition frequently related to nicotine or cocaine abuse. Nicotine had separated me from my values. I smoked even though I knew it was bad for the baby. Nicotine had me. My life is proof that nicotine is a drug and I am a drug addict just as surely as any heroin or cocaine addict.

As the unmanageability of my life began to add up, I realized I needed a Twelve Step program. I was not getting much support from AA or therapy when I discussed quitting. I even had a doctor suggest that I was too depressed to stop smoking. I finally found Nicotine Anonymous and attended meetings weekly. Still I continued to smoke. I tried cutting down to quit, but I don't have the kind of energy it takes to control nicotine. It is too powerful. I smoked and I was totally miserable. I obsessed about smoking and quitting. At one point, I thought I would either have to quit smoking or die because I was in so much pain.

Fortunately, I didn't have to die. My higher power saved me. One night I was out driving and smoking. I was really upset and yelled aloud, "I'm tired of struggling with this (smoking)." Then a "voice" said, "Then why not let it go?" And the urge to smoke was gone – the first time in my smoking career that I was unchained from the compulsion to smoke. I would like to say that I quit there

## She Kept Coming Back

and then, but I was still scared of life without nicotine, so I took the addiction back. At least I knew the way.

I continued to go to Nicotine Anonymous all this time and developed friendships with the members. (I attended meetings for more than two years before I stopped.) I was always welcome although I still smoked. I began to realize that I had made smoking my god, my higher power. It was my "solution" to every problem, every emotion in my life. Sad, angry, happy, broke, scared, sick – I smoked. I also realized that I was terrified of quitting. I began to trust a little in a power greater than myself. Someone at a meeting said she asked for courage and willingness to stop. I did the same and it worked!

I set a quit date for July 18, but I was dragging my feet, afraid of failure. I prayed for guidance. H.P. (Higher Power) gave me a nudge. I had the phone watch for AA on the 17th. In the middle of the night, I had to find someone on the Twelve Step list to call a person back. After about fifteen no answers, I finally reached a man who had lost his larynx and spoke with an amplifier. So there was my guidance from H.P.

I stopped smoking that morning. I used the nicotine patch. It was rough the first three months, but I had the support of the group and H.P. I was depressed and full of rage for a time. My worst fear in quitting was that I would lose my job because I would be emotionally out of control. Well, I did lose my job for a different reason, and I found out that I could survive losing my job. The worst had happened and I didn't have to smoke over it! Furthermore, I found that H.P. provided for me every step of the way.

Today, I have almost two years. I go for days, even weeks without thinking of smoking. I can't stand being around smoke. I'm much calmer now, less depressed, more involved in life. I'm learning how to live a life based on spiritual ideals. I do service work in the program. To me it's vital to stay with Nicotine Anonymous. It saved my life and continues to bless me in so many ways. H.P. gave me, a completely hopeless addict, a miracle – freedom from the compulsion to smoke.

She Kept Coming Back

# A Puff Away

*He used the principles of the program to stop using nicotine before he ever heard of Nicotine Anonymous. Now, smoke free for many years, he continues to attend meetings to insure that he stays free.*

I "smoked" my first cigarette when I was no more than four or five years old. I lived in a project. We played in the courts and streets, would find old butts and "do like the big people do." These early attempts were met by violent coughing, and I don't actually remember ever enjoying a single cigarette or other smoking material.

In my early teen years I didn't really smoke, but to be cool one had to have a pack of smokes rolled up in the sleeve of one's T-shirt. I was probably more self-conscious than the average teen, so I would dig out my pack and carefully roll them in the proper place. They were only a quarter a pack in the machines. (In fact, they were twenty-three cents and the change was inside the cellophane wrapper.) Money was tight and this, coupled with the still present cough reflex, meant that I actually smoked very few of these "precious props" during the period.

During these years, my father was a drinker/smoker and would put his crumpled packs of cigarettes in his bureau drawers when he got home from a night of cards and drinking. These packs provided an auxiliary supply of smokes, but the packs were not available for rolling up in the shirt sleeve as they were all crumpled up. The two or three remaining cigarettes would have to be carefully "uncrumpled" to be used. After smoking (or more accurately, choking) one or two of these treasured butts, I would rush into the house and head straight for the refrigerator and the pickle jar to hide my breath. Dad had a special idea of how to stop us from any bad habit: more of the same. "You think you want to smoke, huh? Well, then, let's see you do it." With this he would provide a pack of cigarettes and light and make me puff on a chain of them until I got sick. I never forgot his yelling and the

## A Puff Away

fear I felt that he would become violent, but it never had any effect on my smoking and choking career.

In my high school years I was involved in the band and smoked little. In 1958, at seventeen years of age, I graduated high school and four days later joined the Navy.

This marks the beginning of my life as a smoker. The company commander was a smoker and would "light the smoking lamp" (an old Navy term left over from the days of wooden ships and iron men) every so often during work details. I would take a break along with the smokers until one day the company commander noticed I was not smoking. He yelled at me to either smoke or get back to work. What a choice! The next day I bought a pack of the mildest cigarettes I could and vowed not to cough in front of my peers. It was tough, but I did okay until someone noticed that I was not inhaling. I was then tutored in the proper technique. I coughed, practiced and became a smoker.

By the time I reenlisted three and a half years later, I was smoking three and a half packs of cigarettes a day. This was no doubt aided by the fact that cigarettes were a dollar a carton on the ship and overseas. But I expect that I would have arrived at this point no matter where I received my training. At this point I first attempted to quit using various methods:

I quit buying them. This lasted only a short while. Most smokers are sympathetic of a fellow smoker who is temporarily out of butts, but when one tries to bum seventy a day, even the most gracious balk

I quit carrying them. I turned my cigarettes over to another smoker with the idea that by having to hunt him down to get one of my smokes, I would have to cut down. Ha ha! Within three days he gave me the remainder of the carton and said I was to quit bothering him every few minutes.

I switched to menthol. I went from three to three and a half packs a day.

## A Puff Away

I gave up trying to quit.

Four years later I was still at this level of use. I was being treated for stomach pain with ulcer medication and would often get up so dizzy after the first smoke of the day that I would have to sit down. There were times I would have to leave work due to nausea in the late afternoon. I never connected any of this to my smoking.

This was before the all-night convenience store, and many a time I would have to dig through the fireplace, the ashtray in the car or the garbage can, to hold me over until the morning. I didn't mind the fireplace or ashtray but hated the ones from the garbage as they were usually wet.

At this time I was teaching a class in Navy school. It was a gentleman's agreement that one could not be bothered while getting ready to smoke a cigarette. This translated into a respite when I was pressed to answer a question for which the answer was not right on the tip of my tongue. The process was: reach in the shirt pocket for the pack; fish one out; tamp it down; open the lighter; put the cigarette in mouth; light the lighter; light the cigarette; inhale slowly; hold it; exhale. This could buy one or two minutes to ponder the answer to the question.

If not for one of the above situations, I might still be smoking. I had opened a fresh pack at eight in the morning and started teaching a class. At half past ten, someone asked a difficult question, and I reached for "old faithful." The pack was empty! I had smoked a whole pack in just more than two hours. This was a real turning point and proved to be the last cigarette I smoked. The package was not even wrinkled. It looked brand new, but it was empty. I realized that I did not *want* the cigarette I was reaching for and could not have wanted the twenty that I had somehow smoked in the previous two and a half hours. I threw the empty pack away and didn't buy another. I would like to say that was the end of my smoking, but that is not the case.

I do not remember any of the details of the withdrawal period, but when I received orders to report to a Navy

## A Puff Away

squadron on its way to Vietnam, my first thoughts were of smoking. How could I face the endless hours at sea waiting for the planes to return from combat without my old pal? It was then I hit on the idea of smoking a pipe. I had smoked a pipe off and on over the years and had one some place. I searched the house and found the pipe and some old tobacco. It was off to the races once again.

I don't know what you know about pipes, but there were two major things that I hadn't thought about. First, a pipe takes a long time to smoke. Second, a pipe is not easy to put out. These issues were to cause me to rethink the whole idea of pipe smoking. I worked on the flight deck close to a lot of aircraft. These aircraft were loaded with bombs, rockets and various forms of fuel. My addiction to nicotine led to the time I was smoking my pipe and was called to the flight deck. I put the pipe in my pocket and ran up on deck. As I ran for the airplane where I was needed, the lit pipe fell out of my pocket and bounced down the deck spewing sparks as it headed for a propeller plane full of high octane aviation fuel. I chased it and caught it just before it reached a small fuel spill. The results could have been disastrous. Nobody seemed aware of how close I was to causing a major fire. I, however, rethought the use of this nicotine delivery system.

That was the last of my pipe smoking days, but once again not of my smoking. I discovered cigars! I always thought of cigar smoking as something rich old men did and never really gave it a thought. As my need for a new nicotine delivery system arose, I bought a box of fifty. Once again, they were cheap on board the ship. I expected a box to last for a month or so. WRONG! I started inhaling them (just as I did the pipe) and rapidly went to eight to ten cigars a day.

Sometime later I was stationed at the U.S. submarine facility in Scotland and hit upon the idea of "cutting down" on the number of cigars I was smoking. Unmindful of my earlier attempts to cut down on cigarettes, I devised a crafty plan. I would only smoke "congratulatory cigars."

## A Puff Away

The hole in this scheme should be immediately apparent to anyone who has served time aboard a Navy ship, particularly in the chiefs' mess. You see, here is a community of several hundred men who are of an age and inclination to father children at an alarming rate. This, plus promotions on a monthly basis, provides an endless supply of "congratulatory" cigars. Couple this with the fact that most men do not really smoke cigars and you have paradise for the likes of a nicotine addict like me. Throughout the chiefs' mess, drawers are always brimming with the remains of the last round of said cigars, available to anyone who wants them. Hence I was able to smoke the required eight to ten cigars per day while keeping my commitment to smoke only those offered to me in a congratulatory way.

During this period, part of my job as the Human Resources Management Specialist was to counsel sailors with alcohol and other drug problems and provide some sort of treatment for them in this isolated area. With this in mind I began attending open Twelve Step meetings with the goal of developing resources for referral. (This was about 1975/76.) Listening to the stories of these individuals, I realized that this program had something wonderful for those who needed it. (The smoke at these meetings was so high that my eyes burned for several hours after attending them.) I realized I could use parts of this simple program to help me stop smoking.

When I stopped, I remember using the Serenity Prayer and the concepts of powerlessness and turning it over with my other daily problems. I do not remember the withdrawal process, but do remember some of the specific things I did to aid me in this successful attempt to finally quit smoking. I stayed away from tobacco/candy shops where I used to stop on my way back from the meetings to buy a pack of cigars. I did not allow smoking in my office aboard the ship. I sat in the back of the room near the door at meetings and went outside for some fresh air when it got too bad. While I don't recommend this, I chewed on wooden coffee stir sticks. (When I retired from the Navy,

I was given a box of five thousand as a gag gift.) I found some other people who did not smoke to confirm that not everyone smoked and that it was okay not to smoke. It would be over ten years before I would be able to see that I had been addicted to a drug and was indeed fortunate to remain drug free.

In July of 1990, I attended my first Nicotine Anonymous meeting. It was a brand-new group and full of newcomers who had no concept of what a Twelve Step program was all about. In spite of this, many accepted the notion that if they had a "desire to remain nicotine free" and would "keep coming back," they would get "smober." In this group I have been able to put a label on the things I did to become and stay nicotine free. Most of all, I realize that I am just one puff away from some three and a half packs or twelve cigars a day.

At one point I was thinking that I would stop attending meetings because "after all it has been over fourteen years since my last smoke." Good old Higher Power intervened and had a friend drop by for a visit. She told me that she had been smoke free for over ten years. She started a new job, was a bit nervous, went into the staff lounge, saw one of her peers take out a pack and on the spur of the moment said, "Can I have one of those?" She is now up to a pack a day and climbing. I have so enjoyed the benefits of being smoke free that I do not want to suffer the same fate, so I choose to continue to attend my insurance policy – Nicotine Anonymous.

# Doing Cancer Research

*The knowledge he acquired as a cancer researcher didn't make it any easier to stop smoking. By practicing the Twelve Steps, he no longer craved nicotine.*

I had to quit smoking <u>again</u>! "Oh Marty," my wife said, "not again. You've quit so many times that I've lost count. Besides, you're always a grouch for a week when you've just quit." I deserved these words of encouragement since they were historically accurate. I had quit many, many times, once for almost two years, but I always went back to smoking.

However, I felt I was not completely powerless over nicotine. If I could go two years without nicotine, I could find a way to control my use: eight to ten cigarettes, or six pipefuls, or three cigars or one chew of tobacco a day. Then I'd be below the Surgeon General's report of lung cancer's incidence and smoking (or in the chewing case, lip cancer). Yet, my new boss was an ex-smoker, a world class cancer researcher and was on that original Surgeon General's commission that linked fifteen or more cigarettes a day and lung cancer (about a third of all cancer deaths). I'd be in agony again for ninety-six hours. Big time cancer researcher!

How had I got into this mess? I started smoking a pipe when I was in high school. It looked hep, just like the TV detective in the early fifties, and they even advertised the brand of pipe tobacco that I chose to smoke. It relieved the stress associated with daily living (and the stress of craving a smoke, but I didn't know that then). By the time I got to graduate school, I was smoking one and a half packs a day, a minimum I didn't fall below for two more decades.

I quit smoking many times. Once I quit, other factors should have influenced my staying quit. In the sixties, my wife and I and our three kids (four eventually) were living in Oklahoma City, OK, and the summer heat required air-conditioning. A closed house with both parents puffing away did not induce a good breathing environment for them or the parents. They complained, but when I tried to quit, I never felt free of the craving for a smoke!

I tried to limit my use to ten cigarettes a day (expensive cigarette case, usually refilled twice more daily). I tried to do the pipe thing (six expensive pipes and tobacco, bitter taste and foul smell). I even chewed tobacco on trips and when outdoors. Anything to get that nicotine in. I couldn't control the amount, and I didn't feel comfortable when not smoking for any extended period (even two years). I must have quit completely (four or more days) fifteen times from 1966 to 1983. I know, for this nicotine addict, the physical craving for nicotine diminishes after about four days; but without a program for living free of nicotine, without spiritual help, the mental craving never goes away. All of this was happening while I was working in cancer research, trying to find a diagnostic marker for liver cancer induced in rats by feeding a chemical carcinogen. We couldn't study lung carcinogenesis; the rats were too smart to start smoking.

Finally, in 1982, my new supervisor was an ex-smoker. It wouldn't do to be the only smoker on his team of more than ten investigators and ten assistants. Fate intervened in that I joined the granddaddy Twelve Step program two months after quitting smoking again. I began to study and tried to practice the Steps. It was obvious that to take any of that drug, alcohol, would readdict me and so I could see I must not take even one cigarette (or nicotine gum or later, nicotine patch), or I would be readdicted to active craving for nicotine. Several months later, I asked my temporary sponsor if I couldn't also add a prayer in the morning, "not to 'need' a smoke today." He said, "You smoke?" He knew what I did for a living. I replied that like other mood altering drugs, knowledge of nicotine addictiveness did not help the addict to stop with serenity. Being a good insurance lawyer, my sponsor said, "Why don't you just say that prayer after the one for sobriety, and use it like a rider on your life insurance policy?" I started doing that on a daily basis and have done it each day-at-a-time for more than twelve years. I ceased craving nicotine shortly after doing what he suggested.

In 1994, I decided that I also needed service work for nicotine addiction, or due to increased living pressures, I was in danger of going back to smoking. I joined a fledgling Nicotine Anonymous group, where by the grace of God, I could join others who haven't "needed" a smoke today. Now, by practicing the other ten Steps, I can finally keep growing up, in the presence of loving friends who are also working this program. Keep it simple.